A Day At A Time
In Rhyme

by
Jane Clifton

A Day At A Time – in Rhyme
Jane Clifton

Littlefox Press
PO Box 816
Kyneton VIC 3444

Author website at
www.janeclifton.com.au

Copyright©2019 Jane Clifton
ISBN - 978-0-6480838-6-3

Cover design and layout by Cassis Lumb

No part of this publication may be re-sold, hired out, reproduced, stored in a retrieval system or transmitted in any form or by any means without the prior written consent of the author and the publisher.

FOREWORD

In 2018, for reasons I will never fully understand, I made a new year's resolution to write a poem every day. I'd written poetry before, but I would not call myself a poet. Nevertheless, I decided to do it. I like a challenge. In 2014 I made a resolution to stop drinking alcohol for a year and nearly died of boredom: once I start something I have to see it through.

Every night - before bedtime and long after wine o'clock - I would sit or lie sprawled on the couch, my grey, Palomino Blackwing 602 pencil poised above the pages of an old desk diary rendered blank by the advent of iCal, and scribble, erase and scrawl. When the poem felt right, felt finished, I would uncap my fountain pen and Moleskin notebook, ink it in, date it, then give it a title. Always in that order.

Short poems - usually a page, occasionally two or three. I fell into a nightly rhythm with the process. Some days it was easy: others, blood out of a stone. Some days four or five ideas would spurt forth: others, particularly towards the end of the year, I'd find myself 'owing' up to 3 or 4 days-worth.

Themes emerged: drinking, performing, friends, family, war and peace, footy, dogs, flowers, my lost son. It was not a diary but some days were acknowledged – Fathers' Day, Mothers' Day, Easter, Christmas, the day Sisto Malaspino was stabbed by a madman in Bourke Street.

For some time now I have been taking photographs of found objects. The idea of including them was irresistible.

january...

January 1st
GOODBYE TO ALL THAT

two or three longnecks
in a paper sack
hidden in plain sight
between the bins
no bugger'll nick 'em
they'll be right
in these milk and bread delivery days
of trust and crust

Merry Christmas, garbos!
hard men of the truck
thanks for the dirty work
amongst spider and fly
collecting our rubbish
without blinking an eye

tipping the men from the tip
with beer
good times
there'll be cheers
at the depot divvy-up tonight.

goodbye to all that
all that sentimental crap.

January 2nd
DEM BOIDS!

birds flying home to roost
such a racket
then not a peep
no Netflix for them
no Foxtel or Stan
no ABC news or emails to scan
no dishes to stack
or pots to scour
no shrink-wrapping leftovers
no wine by the hour
no beds to turn down
stories to read
alarms to set
dogs to feed
twittering and tweeting
cawing and shrieking
ducking and diving
in-formation
as if in frustration
at this nightly curfew
ally ally in!
all along the branch line
until the light is gone
and the tree is quiet.

January 3rd
16 ACROSS*

TOP DRESSES
I've worn?
TOP DRESSES
the front lawn?
top dresses?
possibly six
ones I can fix
by letting out
never in
never thin again
was I ever?
no I never
was
because
of my top in dresses
look where the seam's torn
wide as the back lawn
my memory
undresses.

January 4th
QUEEN OF SHEBAH

girls in cars
on the way home
from bars
in my car
they are
laughing, joking
slurring, blurring the lines
between friendship
and wine
they had such a good time
good thing that I'm
driving them
to where they are
safe.

---

* Decision: to take my poetry topic from the answers to The Age cryptic crossword of the day (but not always)

January 5th
11 ACROSS: FAN CLUB

I'm in the fan club
big fan of fanclubs, me
more generally
a fan of fans
when heat waves
and north winds fan the flames
of desire
for coolth.
gimme a lolloping punkah
in my roof
a whirling set of blades
slicing through wattage
on the gauge.
flip me a pleated half-moon
lace-edged or lacquered
loosely stitched, tattered
or paper!
paper will do
any old sheet
seconds to pleat
and flutter through the heat
with your palm
I'm a fan
of the fan.

January 6th
42°

slow-cooking in our houses
while Niagara freezes shut
porky pigs we are,
north wind playing wolf
salted crackling by the aircon
dreaming snowflake long agos
when there were four seasons
times to believe in
not these bumpy bouts
of mother nature in her menopause
all hot flushes and mood swings
and nothing to look forward to
but
lights out
power down and
another big bang.

January 7th
SEE SEE 20:20

spirit level in my eye
detects height
he might
be you.
No.
too wide, short, ugly
but maybe
No.
not you
when it is you
everything falls into line
it could be no one else but
your body
is else
where.

January 8th
4 ACROSS: MY WORD

my word
they're all
my word
I have
no word
to express my love of
my, my, my
(I can do better than this)
I have words
at my fingertips
words at my toes
wherever I goes
on the tip of the
tongue
on the drum
of the ear
behind the eye
beneath the mind
above the spirit
beside the point
next door to reason
slave to the brain
explain
again
on the line of the page
my words
make it clear
my word
they do.

January 9th
A RARE SIGHTING OF OUR SON

Corkscrew through my heart
turning turning
Acid in my gut
burning burning
Why are you so mean?
What does it all mean?
turning turning
burning burning
Worse than the pain
of bringing you forth
when I was sane
and you were all the world
to us
in a hanky
now all is pus
and spleen
and ache
watered in vitriol
pickled in spite
of our love
and all wrong
is right
without
you.

January 10th
TAP TAP

shuffle hop knock
ball change
I shoulda kept up with the tap dancing
I still got the shoes
and the taps
and the nails
not the moves
not the sail
or the glide
I got rhythm all right
but not that kind
that slips by the mind
heads straight to
the feet
reet-per-teet
snippitty snap
tippitty tap
shazam!
my knees mighta stood
a fair chance
if I'da stuck
with the dance.

January 11th
A SCREAM

the kettle screams
and I don't care
who hears it
wake the house
upset the dog
scatter the birds
banish the cat
slam the neighbour's door.
when making tea it's
whistling time down
to its own breathy tune
how about a nice cuppa
shutthefuckup
all you jug time-juggling
teabag dunkers
snapchat wankers
instagram stalkers
texting walkers
tweeting twits
facebook shits
there is time
to simmer
and to steam
and dream
and scheme
there is time
for leaves
and cosie
teacup rosy
there is time
to whistle
steam.

January 12th
ALL IN ALL

have I peaked?
have I hit the wall?
is today the day?
I can't write anything
but scrawl
me and my lists
me and my goals
me and my standards
me and my big ideas
all programmed to fall
at the first
and yet
I shall steel myself
(and put myself back)
and words will come
to me
see?
I got it done…

January 13th
THE BIG DRY

two weeks dry
without a drink
I'm liking this
I think.
I love the red
I love the glass in hand
I love the drop
the fall from real
the lack of feel
the fuckyouIdon'tcare
swagger
I'm so grown-up that
I could almost smoke!

I love the license
and the easy words
the need to dance
the right to weep
the coma
and the public snore
the nerve to bore
then creep
between sheets
and curse the glass
and curse the red
and toss and turn
all night in my hot bed
that brings no sleep

only the constant need to pee
and check the pulse
and check the time
and count the hours
'til daylight

the dry is good
the dry's a bore
there's no relief from
brutal
banal
real
it's all feel, feel, feel,
unmitigated feel
unpeeled
awake
alert
for too much thinking time
too much mind
if you don't mind

but dry is good
it is
I just know
no
is best.

January 14th
JEFFERSON STARSHIP SANG

'have you seen the stars tonight?'
what?
in the sky?
no, I
looked at the others
that scroll across my screen
to tell me what will be
or not be
foretelling me beware
take care
and be aware of other signs
and try not to shoot my mouth off
like others of my months
are wont to do
no,
that won't do
at all.

guidance
from the stars
I have not viewed tonight
a-sparkle in their dark and velvet home
no, I
don't like to look
in case I see
where
and who
I am.

January 15th
AND THEN

here I am
in the swirl
of wine
of why
do I
do it?

I couldn't help myself
couldn't take it
up against the wall
of pain
of hurt
no,
that's not true.

I'm just
weak
face it.

January 16th
MOLLY ROSE TO THE WORLD

little girl flying
through the great big sky
to the world
just like you flew
through me
to be born
well, not so much
flew
as grew
through me
to the world.

flying free
of me
and everybody you love
and everybody who loves you back
and you'll be back
but it won't be you
you'll be new
fresh-minted by the world
little girl
flying through the great big sky
to the new.

January 17th
(D)JA(K)NÖ(W)ME?

a stitch in time
saves nine
but I can't seem
to stop at seams
the lines and lines and lines
of needle tacking
thread through cloth
and fabricating
shape
and sleeve
and leg
and collar
skirt and dart and
snip snip snip
and
pin pin pin
clipping corners
spooling twine
hemming edges
marking time.

January 18th
5 DOWN: ACCURACY

accuracy
I like it
plain and simple
to the point
no flannel
fluff or flummox
or bog plain lack of skill
I like it
to a fault
one ought to make an effort
put in some thought
get it right
and delight
to execute
and to receive
a cup of crystal clarity
of steel-cut purpose
and intent
exactly
precisely what one meant
to say.

January 19th
CAN DO WILL DO CANTO

those who can
do
those who can't
teach
but can can doers
teach?
can teachers
do?
I am a doer
who ought to have taught
I am a doer who can
does that mean
I have run out
of things I can do?
except for the things
I have learned how to teach?
does that mean
I can
know how
to show
how
to do?

January 20th
THE HACK'S LAMENT

dodged another bullet
phew!
they didn't find me out
see through me
call my bluff
ask to see my papers
my ID, CV, B-I-Oh
that way they'd know
if I had any right
to be
up there
making out
like I know
the how, the why, the what-to-do
who, me?
what would I know?
what do I know?
they will never know
I will never know
when
to just admit
I do know
some shit.

January 21st
FUNEREAL

saying goodbye
ouch!
I'm here to help
to do it right
because
there is a right way
and an oh-so-wrong
seen enough of that old play
all the praying
all the gongs
there should be
dignity
and panic and some fear
and tears
a laugh or two
and beer
asparagus rolls
something comforting
a mother's smile
beaming from a spool of family snaps
from then to this sad place
and every memory cherished
put to bed
just the way we'd like it
for ourselves.

**January 22nd
CHAT**

and there you are
left of screen
a spot of green
on line you are
so far away
can't say 'hey'
no more
almost forgotten
lost the plot it seems
no connection
just the faintest buzz
of what was
for me
a tiny breath of life
of hope
in a crisp white cotton tee.

January 23rd
ANTONIA

we shall gather
'neath the trees
to say goodbye
and everyone will ask the question
why
the father and the mother
the sister and the lover
the children and the friends
the painters and the singers
the thinkers and the drinkers
the faces of confusion
the utter desolation
the waste, the loss
the what-the-fuck and
why
did she die
and I will try my best
to steer them through
the dark and icy cataracts
of grief
into that brief,
calm, restful
harbour
of
okay.

January 24th
HEIDE HO

dappled light on rugs
the forest floor
the living/room
silver branch
green leaf windmill
spinning spinning
lifted by the softest breeze
god's breath
like summer should be
friendly
peace in a park
not these boiling, raging days
of blinding haze
of ten ton torpor
shattered slumber
pitch and toss
on burning sheets
and foetid pillows
soft summer in a park
kind, gentle summer
loosening arms
and faces
opening hearts
to hope
and faith and
glory be
nothing but blue skies
from now on.

January 25th
10 ACROSS: KNAPSACK

I love to go
a-wandering
across the world and back
and as I go
I love to sing
that's all there is to that.

burning feet below my desk
are itching to be gone
over the hills
and far away
but never to Hong Kong
or Bali or the home of phō
or any place that's steamy
give me blizzards!
ice and snow
I don't find drizzle dreary.

trapped inside my bank account
there's no way outta here
no plane to catch
no trip to book
no fond farewells
or jet-lag socks
no passport check-in
shoes to pack.

safe inside suburbia
the same thing
everyday
I had my polyglottal fun
globe-trotting
yesterday
I waved my hand
and yodelled loud
my knapsack on my back.

January 26th
NADA NADIR

the tyranny of structurelessness
that's what we used to say
at close of play
in fuck-all days
the hours unfurl now
merciless
with no agenda
I am
my own woman
doing and
not doing and
waiting watching
for results
approval
worth
respect
and worse
sitting wide
on my flat arse
filling my midriff
with hard lard
skipping hard yards
hoping
to be used
I will never get used
to doing nothing
well.

**January 27th
MORNING**

sometimes
methinks
I could just lay me down
to sleep all day
the torpor
is seductive
I was productive
I gave good show
but they
will take their own sweet selfish time
to pay
and I
am unproductive
'til they do
hemmed in
gridlock
running out of spark
to start anew
and my bed calls
and my soft e-bay chair
'come to us you melancholy baby'
waste more time
pillowed up in listlessness
beside the silent phone
of inactivity
ad nauseum
ad hoc
ad lib
ad infinitum.

NIGHT

there is pleasure
to be had
at the wheel of my car
driving
far far far
round and round the town
up Sydney
down Brunswick
round Docklands
to the sea
singing along
with The Beatles
in harmony
shooting the shit with the ladies
A.K.A. 'pax'
picking up dropping off
mostly it's driving
and driving
and singing with Joni
past queues for gigs
and all the kids are chiacking
and flirting and texting
drinking and swaying
on these hot nights
of their very own
summer of love
all long hair
and high heels
and squeals
and not a ciggie in sight
on these damp, sexy nights
of their youth
dewpoint 35
and it's good
to be alive.

January 28th
METAPHYSICAL HAIR*

metaphysical hair
that's what I need
to fill the patches
of my self-destructive
autonomous immunity.
bald spots
liver spots
as by Lot, God wot:
that's what I've got
got off lightly, you'd assay
in the stakes of age
so far, to guage
wrinkle-free, health
no wealth
and a dearth of love
here at the business end
you'll get no complaints
from me
while I can still walk
and eat
and shit
and breathe
and wee
no peep out of me
except about the hair
the physical lack of hair
metaphysical in its despair.

---

*Ad for a company of this name seen on the Mystic Medusa website

January 29th
NOW THAT THE RAIN IS FALLING

to sleep
perchance to sleep
that'd be a plus.
once so simple
now my bed is hard
as old Procrustes' rack
and dreamtime
is a wake-up call
that chimes upon the hour
to signal
pillow relocation
side to side
kneecap elevation
on my back
facedown, hands down
out of the question
no suggestion
of relief
of eight hours deep
did I ever
do eight hours straight?
yes
when I was eight
for lights out
in Bedfordshire
and a goodnight kiss
bliss.

January 30th
IN THE ZONE

the super moon
draws the tides
th'eclipse will hide
its face
and blush it pink as a girl
traffic snarls
tempers boil
passions flare
hearts uncoil
and run around like bats
in hats
laughing at trees
smiling at thieves
no one believes all that
until they put out the cat
last thing at night
to see what once was bright
all in a rosy glow
and hear puppies barking
at the sky.

January 31st
IN THE PINK AND BLUE AND SUPER

no wonder
humans had to make up
god
how else could they explain
a sky like that?
the great white ball
forever changing shape
has suddenly turned pink!?
Oh. Em. Gee.
what else were they supposed to think?
it had to mean
something
it couldn't simply
be.

it's silent out there now
no wind to stir the trees
the stars
are ranked about
the gay pink moon
in awe
in silent, gobsmacked wonder
at the trick
of such a wondrous
godless
sight.

we are hanging
in the universe and
the moon is
playing possum with the sun
ducking
behind our earthly skirts
we are
so small
and in great need of god
o, if only there was one
to make sense
of all
this wonder.

**February 1st
WANING**

I know how the moon feels
tonight
yesterday's superstar
in the spotlight
every neck
craning for a view
of beautiful
clever
important
impressive
celestial
luminary
you.

ta-dah!
no need to say
'look at me', moon
folks journeyed miles
for a view
they were willing to
pay
to gaze
upon your marvellous cosmic
loveliness
at your once-in-a-lifetime
glow
to ooh and ah at the
show.

'But hey, world!'
I hear you moan, moon
'you fickle bunch of fucks
I'm still up here!
I've still got it!
I'm bigger and clearer
tonight
there are steps
on the Maribyrnong
right
up to my door
I am
luscious pearl and shimmering
and, I believe,
better than before!'

no, moon
no one's out of doors tonight
with telescopic lenses
in Instagrammatic frenzies
old news
sweet moon
Thursday's featherduster, you
losing face
in outer space
where nobody
can hear you
scream.

February 2nd
TATTOO

contemplating ink
I think about it
all the time
I want it written
on my skin
but not for all to see
a private mark
a scar
words from the bard
to soothe my soul
outward sign of an inward pain
reverse sacrament
written testament
but not to flash around
like some old trendy trashy moll
and yet
I crave it
stalk the shop
crack head chasin'
needle on skin
but not in
and
ink like blood
shall flow from
my old broken heart
'Grief fills the room up of my absent child.'
I want it written
on my skin.

February 3rd
OH, YES! JOLIE POITRINE!

we big titters
never get the lead
our busts condemn us
to play nurses,
strippers, madames, bullies,
headmistresses, fishwives,
harridans and sluts
pornographic proportions
will not play
house
or fall in love
be loved
perform heroic feats
have their day in court
fly solo round the world
or to the moon
or fit into designer frocks
our teats define us
make our figures fun
as if we chose
this sagging profile
as if we wanted underwiring
craved the cleavage
that demeans us
as if we made it happen
or didn't do enough
to make it stop
as if we didn't have
a brain up top
o, blessed be the flat of chest
for they shall be
no trouble at all
nor take up any space
that's more than
small
blessed be the A cup
and the B
for they shall have
whatever
they
want.

February 4th
SUNDAY NIGHT WRITE

a little pome
sans fuss
a Sunday pome
because I must
continue what I started
resist fainthearted
no drinking
daily poetry
seem like two good ideas
to me.

February 5th
NIGEL

heartbreak of day
my son still away
another year ticks by
another hour, another minute
absence makes the heart grow dry
and cracked
to think he's never coming back.

a good man died
too soon
doing what he loved,
swimming
leaving us to flail about
in a sea of bullshit.
a bad mad quit
and that should be good news
but is it?
another man will take his place
another wrecker of the race.

two families
shared their grief with me today
that's how I earn my keep
and Nigel,
the world's loneliest bird,
has died beside the decoy girl
he loved
to death

lured onto a barren isle
to breed a new flock
with a concrete block
Nigel loved that cold and heartless chick
preened stony feathers
built a fragile nest
expected nothing
and got nothing in return.

O, Nigel, Nigel!
my heart breaks
in waves of sorrow
upon the cruel and jagged shoreline
of our heartbreak day.

**February 6th
WHO?**

cracks the chiropractor's back
drills the dentist's teeth
trims the hairdresser's fringe
waxes the depilator's minge
paints the manicurist's nails
grills the chef's entrails
scrubs the skivvy's floor
makes love to the whore
pleads the lawyer's case
lifts the surgeon's face
rubs the masseur's neck
bounces the banker's cheque
parks the valet's car
returns a mother's unconditional love
protects the soldier's home
brews the barista's joe
hears the priest's confession
entertains the clown
rescues the lifeguard
tunes the mechanic's car
lies to the politician
safeguards the nanny
surprises the florist
snares the angler

shoots the hunter
shames the gossip
mystifies the sleuth
swindles the gyp
cheers on the sports fan
books the grey ghost's van
keeps the copper in line
calls the innkeeper's time
shushes the librarian
corrects the grammarian
impresses the astronaut
frightens the spook
throws knives at the cook
mows Jim's lawn
delivers the midwife's newborn
checks the optician's sight
puts every wrong to right
inters the undertaker
buries the gravedigger
who
wipes away
the celebrant's tears.

February 7th
SEND YOUR CAMEL TO BED

my neighbour's pool
is perfect deep
after midnight
these hot sleepless nights
I crab my way across the street
a shadow in a hooded towel
to slip the catch
and trip the lights
to wallow
in the lovely shallows slated there
to float
beneath the palm tree fronds
and navy velvet sky
of stars
as bats flap by
a possum stirs
the dog attempts a listless growl
too hot to guard
this cool suburban hollow, this oasis
fat pink unicorns and
toady rubber rings
glide past and eye
my dunking, cooling frame
of legs and arms
no longer aflame
or awash with steamy sweat
I lie in the bliss
of absolute
wet.

February 8th
MISSING IN ACTION

I don't miss sex at all
should I?
I do miss singing once a week
to five or ten
or thirty-two
to strut my midnight creep
I miss the grooves
the moves
the glass in hand
my three-piece band
and even getting paid
I don't miss getting laid
at all
O, but I do miss kissing
that's what I been missing
it must be years
since I was kissed
between the ears
more than a peck
something reckless, bliss
or held
or gently touched
or felt
a little loved
if I could still
sing once a week
I'd sing
The Thrill Is Gone.

February 9th
THRENODY

like two funerals in one day*
two funerals in one day
'smiling as the shit comes down'
dealing with
both sides of pain
the mother
and the lover
and the daughter
and the scion
beneath a cruel sun
hard up
against a stony son
can't get my sorry
work done
'blood dries up
like rain, like rain'
won't bring them back
not even
two funerals in one day
words are all I have
to say
at two funerals in one day.

---

* Apologies to Crowded House

February 10th
I DIDN'T SAY THEY WOULD BE GREAT POEMS

thank pharmacy
for Panadol
to lull my throbbing head
a timely balm
to cure the urge
to drink myself to bed.

February 11th
MORNING SONG

black gut
twisted dreams
breath of death
hello day
cancer
that's what it is
cancer
of the stomach
of the gullet
of the throat
of the liver
no way can it just be
dull dyspepsia
how dare you fault my
hypochondria
I know a symptom
when I feel it
a change of heart
will not conceal it
I fall apart
with each black morning after
by tonight
I'll be alright
after today
I'll be okay.

February 12th
UP FROM THE SKY

mackerel sky over Knifepoint
I pause for a pic
and a think –
there must have been
thrilling skyscapes
before now
how come everyone's on Insta
snapping
sunsets and roses
beaches and birds
like my mother used to do?
where are all the people, ma?
your camera
is only lining up roses
no people pose in
your still life.

and she would smile
a secret smile
of knowing
just how hard it is
to catch life in a jar
like some exotic jam

my sky
is shocking pink now
Wedgewood blue
purple, silver, primrose, too
Raphael Turner Dali
streaking Maxfield Parish tricks
cross heaven
as the world powers down
to the last big flash
in the frying pan.

there must have been
glorious skies like this
before
when my Mary Quant eyes were
fixed
upon the floor.

February 13th
THIS MAY APPEAR MORE THAN ONCE

in the begging line
marking time
waiting for the buck
to stop
the penny
to drop
I hit the marks!
I said the words!
I gave good show!
I made them laugh!
and now it's time to pay
me
don't delay
please
I am jogging on the spot
in the begging line
for all time
in the begging line.

February 14th
ST FLORIST'S DAY

crush of roses
pink and scarlet
spilling from a seashell vase
like foam upon the lip
of strawberry creamy
concha china
rippled and ribbed
curving out to a bell
trumping up
to cup the fragrant spray
forever caught on film
beautiful still
sweet reminder
of some perfect day
of scented garden
happy home
and friendship
marked by leaf and cutting
sewn deep into my yard
a hint of you
a touch of your green thumb
a pot upon a stair
fall of cactus hair
keeps memory
in bloom.

February 15th
DESIGN FOR LIVING

people writing books of rules
to tell us how to live
people buying books of rules
paper rafts
bobbing on a sea of life
they cannot fathom
on their own
matchstick beacons
in the pea soup fog
of terror
of the dark
unknown
what separates the greedy
from the needy?
the chancer
from the thirst for answers?
the more-front-than-Myers
nerve
to offer solutions
absolution at a price?
from the fatal need for advice
in this mortal confusion
this fallen paradise
these unfulfilled ambitions
need for contrition
and a moment's peace.

February 16th
PARAMOUNT POSE(UR)

balancing
on one leg
right arm straight ahead
wing
left arm straight behind
wing
I am flying
out across the lake
below the sky
I am swan
I am weightless, graceful
high
ducking down
and to the side
I glide
Neneh's 7 Seconds
Youssou N'Dour
'beaucoup de sentiments'
toujours l'amour
violins weeping lament
in my ear
and you're near
I'll be waiting
I'll be waiting
for you dear
as if time has stood still
and there was something
to wait for
all alone in my hoodie
hard by the lake shore
on one pin
I am flying flying flying
in the gym
balanced and poised
thinking of you
still.

February 17th
PHILISTINES-R-US*

white night, big city
gone to my hipster head
White Knight, big chewie
I'd rather stay home in bed
wish they'd spent the dollars
on something useful instead

walking and walking
to look at some lights?
I'd rather look at the walls
(architecture must surely be
the most insulted artform of all)
white night
nuit blanche
tram on in from the burbs
it's so very French
to join
heaving humanity
gawping at art
moving at snail's pace
from food truck to park
on Chinese New Year
there be dragons and dogs
and crackers
and puppets
and rappers
and mimes
you'll be so entertained
you'll be out of your mind
on this
white night, hip city
I'd rather stick pins in my head
White Knight, hard chewie
I'd rather suck that instead.

---

*apologies to Jimmy Reed and, possibly, The Animals

February 18th
EGG AND CHIPS

egg and chips
on Sunday night
lazy dinner
guilty delight
baked beans, too
runny yolk amongst the sauce
toasty fingers licking off
a simple course
for one
beside the box
a bonnet drama
Skandi noir
and frenzied knitting
bears
to pass the time
without the wine
to blur the line
between
night and day
between
one week and another
between
now and when
egg and chips
on Sunday night
with my sweet mother
was sublime.

February 19th

SEA FEVER by John Masefield

I must go down to the seas again to the lonely sea and the sky
And all I ask is a tall ship and a star to steer her by;
And the wheel's kick and the wind's song and the white sail's shaking
And a grey mist on the sea's face, and a grey dawn breaking.

I must go down to the seas again, for the call of the running tide
Is a wild call and a clear call that may not be denied;
And all I ask is a windy day with the white clouds flying,
And the flung spray and the blown spume and the sea-gulls crying.

I must go down to the seas again, to the vagrant gypsy life,
To the gull's way and the whale's way where the wind's like a whetted knife;
And all I ask is a merry yarn from a laughing fellow-rover,
And quiet sleep and a sweet dream when the long trick's over.

JOHN MASEFIELD SAID

'I must go down to the seas again'
I thought it was just to 'the sea'
'to the lonely sea and the sky'
says John
but the sea could be having a party
the sea could be having friends over
the sky may lower
upon us with ill will
but I need to see the sea soon
or my soul will surely die.

born on a rock
cast between two oceans
born with salt spray in my lungs
the need for me to see the sea
is how my wheel is sprung

'for the call of the running tide
is a wild call….that may not be denied'
says John
it's primal, to the bone
I need ozone, vasty blue
and frothy, creamy foam.

in my igloo
on the shore
shaded from the rays
like King Canute
I'll fix my gaze
upon that lovely, endless sea
then take a lungful
dip my toes
and croon a hymn of praise.

February 20th
HAND TO THE WHEEL

tiny movements
minute tics
a blink, a wink
no time to think
automatic
auto pilot
George is in control
of heart and lung and brain
and skin
and nails that take a month to grow
by slow degrees
a sneeze, a cough
a wheeze
the breeze that shakes the leaf
the hair, the skirt
the flying dirt
the sun, the stars, the moon
perpetual motion
popping corn
a child is born
a new day dawns
a sheep is shorn
no time to mourn
and life goes on
in tiny movements
little thoughts
heartbeats, footsteps
hiccups, burps
sunbeams dancing on the lawn.

February 21st
SLOTH

the lazy drag
against the gym
(turn the wheel!
o, go back home!)
reluctance to pick up the pen
(play with Facebook!
and your phone!)
inertia
it's a powerful force
magnetic
it could kill a horse
but horses don't need
sit-ups
push-ups
those steeds don't have to
tread the mill
pump the iron
wield the quill
to make some sentence
tell a tale
that maybe no one wants
to read
that no one's asking
to be writ

O, waste more time!
procrastinating
why, oh, why
all this creating
and this drive to be
gyrating
in pursuit of fit
a little bit
of slim

O, turn the wheel!
go back home!
tweet a little!
tap that phone!
surrender to the lazy drag
put up your feet
you
fat old bag.

February 22nd
ON SEEING THE BEAUTIFUL

I feel the earth move
people leap to their feet
to cheer the sweet familiar
feels good, so right
is worth the price
of admission
and free tonight
duelling spotlights
flashing teeth
risky heels
Ladies queues
fast drinks at intermission
remember that one?
la-la-la la-la
play me more
I love that tune!
I feel secure
I am being entertained
I ask for nothing more
play me all the notes I like
solid gold
reliable
money in the bank
all I need's a bar or two
a wig, a sequin, high-heeled shoe
I'll rise up from my velvet pew
to stomp the floor
and encore you
ticketty ticketty boo.

February 23rd
LOVE IN SWEDEN (STOCKHOLM SYNDROME)

trolleys rolling two by two
flat-pack dating is in swing
rack and six-pack
diamond ring

will he linger by the duvets
fitted queen sheets fingering
candles can be sexy, too
she's not taken with those cushions
he's not dazzled by desk lights
eyes are flashing out a signal
wonder if he's free tonight

should she ask him
would she dare
thrust a trolley in his path
she stretched out wide to check a sofa
can't believe she's gone so far

wait a minute
he's with someone
they're both checking out a bath
loading towels, fluffy throws
toothmugs, pegs, a shower rose
his and his
they could be twins
matching tees and shorts and Vans
trim moustaches, ear-ring studs
heart tattoos, rimless glasses

she finds herself at Bargain Corner
NQR will be her thing
trolleys filling, two by two
flat-pack mating is the thing.

February 24th
MRS IBSENSON

I'm writing a play
got carried away
today
it flowed from my hand
in a rush
'til I cramped up
full-stop
for a breather
a pizza, a wine
I'm a believer
in riding the wave
as it rolls
through your arm
to the page
'til it stops at your brain
and you can't find
one more line
to explain
all the thoughts in your head
all the shapes
and the sizes
the laughs and surprises
in store
and you bless their arrival
like children
like freshly baked cakes
like sweet-smelling roses galore.

February 25th
RIOT TV

fitted llama waistcoat
flares
badly cut hair
the scent of patchouli
fair rolls off the screen
and I am back
in old Balmain
scrawled slogans on walls
straight
out of our heads
playing at reds
swapping beds
standing up
for ideas
in our jeans
and our op-shop gear
bra-less and free
Honda 50
born to be wild
in a world of
absolute rule
and Camus
only a fool
took it up to a horse
and a rider
with all of the force
of the law on his side

a paddy wagon ride
a beating
a strategy meeting
us and them
now and then
way back when
in a pre-colour world
of black and white
sharp and clear
original
despite fear
we were working it out
we were up for
the struggle the cause
and the blood and the guts

I'd forgotten it
some of it
so long ago
and then
there it was on my screen
an old friend
in high resolution
the old revolution
so simple, so clear
where you stood
yesteryear.

February 26th
AUTODIDACT

always dive straight in
never prep
never study
never cram
just do
see it and think
why not?
no.

go for broke
(always broke)
pencil to the page
foot upon the stage
hand up for the crack
be all right, Jack
lips to the mic
on the night
suck the lights

nothing ventured
who's to blame
no sense shrinking
from the game
when there's so much
to be gained
no sense in restraint
no one to blame
but you.

February 27th
HUNTSMAN

spider on my wall
long and hairy
thick
but not so furry
brown jelly legs
up close, in fact
I don't fear you at all
but I can't share my
room with you
I won't play host
to your arachnid sprawl

you have to go
let me fetch the jar
the slice of card
we won't travel far
let me relocate you
in the yard
to find another lair
in which to trap your fare

I forgive you
I'm not cross
the wind has blown you
off your track
into the house
I won't kill you
but you have to face the fact
Hunter
this room is not a home
for both of us
don't make a fuss
you have to go.

**February 28th
MOO!**

the call comes
another shot
another sniff
of where the cherry is
another chance
to walk the walk
talk the talk
hit the marks
make the charts
roll the dice
ha!

the call comes
but not for you
that deal is done
the dotted line is signed
but still you jump
like Pavlov's dog
the hook is in your mouth
you'll learn the lines
try to impress
slyly assess
the competition
waiting with you
for a chance
to shine
to make their mark
have one more dance

the call comes
it's from New York!
you can't believe it
and it's for a lead!
you can't wait to read
to learn those lines
to find out
if they'll see you
really

when disappointment comes
this time
(as surely it will do)
it will be international
and that's something
new.

March 1st
"TO AUTUMN"

this is it
the wall
full moon
March 1st
antipodean 'Fall'
and nothing
at all
but a red stain
at the bottom of an empty glass
and late night cornbread
pickling
my insides.

March 2nd
PARTY POOPER

the party's over
for the pretty balloon
to burst or blow
the jumbo off course
fun time is over
for the party balloon
but how will we know
where the wedding is?
the garage sale
the twenty-first?

the world's a safer place
without beautiful balloons
but how will we know
how to celebrate?
without bubbles of air
or helium
that's running out, too
so jolly unfair
how will we welcome
the newborn baby?
comfort the sickly
say happy birthday?

it's goodbye to balloons,
confetti and glitter
all of it
nothing but
glorified litter.

March 3rd
TALKING STICK

'pass ag'
meaning?
seems mean
to hurl it my way
sideways snide
mid-chat
as if somehow to sum me up
as if somehow to say
I don't get the play
it shut me up
was that the point?
okay.
have it your way

'shift response'
(back to me)
shift 'focus'? 'manoeuvre'?
that came my way, too
as if I wasn't there
on that chair
right where
I thought friends were at

so pretentious
pop psycho-anal-isis
why not just
'shut your hole, mole'
and be done
I can take it
I'll help you tie the gag
but then
oops!
that's what they call
'pass ag'.

March 4th
CAMPASPE

riverbank tree
at an angle bent and
all is still
in the peppercorn air
geese in a crocodile
up bank
headed for the pub
hooligan cockatoos
swoop and shriek
above the dirt brown curvy creek
sculpted mud walls
tower and loom
mouldings carved in concave earth
expose dark roots
like sinews
arteries
veins stripped from bank flesh
freeze frame
flash flood
after shock
gnarled and grievous bodily land
timeless white bark
pocked and graceful
old gum ladies proud and wise
congregate beneath a warm
blue sky
at sun's
slow
down.

March 5th
OP SHOPPING

poking through yesterdays
in search of
new now
swaying racks of
his and her dross
in search of
wow
through a prism of hip
gold at the tip
rifle the murk
stifle the
sour dusty smell
memories and death
stonewashed dreams
of glamour
success
in a brown crochet dress.

March 6th
SISTERS

eenie meanie mynee moh
who will be the first
to go
of us four
who will make it three
or two
or less
we are locked in
for now but
the finish line
draws close
odds shorten
scars open
wounds will not heal
hair will not re-grow
bones never mend
knees will not bend
again

we lost the first
in such a rush
no time to think
of us
as us
loose litter of mismatched cats
Siamese and tabby
Persian and mog
no dog
to yardstick by

I spied what might be
with my little eye
tonight
and took fright
at the sight
of
The End.

March 7th
THE SWIMMING POOL

stroking the blue
carving the cool
navy T-stripe
of the pool
ageless
timeless
weightless
boneless
careless
lap to lap to lap to lap
to twenty, forty
up and back
in restful effort
afloat
in the sac
of life
liquid and free
head over heel
in the deep
I am twelve
I am six
eleven and five
alive
and wet
and me.

March 8th
SUMMER NIGHT VIEWING

in the treehouse
with the screen
Fahrenheit 451
except
it doesn't see me
yet
that will come
it will vet
my every thought and deed
that won't amount to much
so out of touch
I'll be
from real
life glimpsed through café glass
or street lines
queuing up for fun
while I align
remote controls
in perfect symmetry

outside
the tree's alive
with bats and rats
shrieking possums on the tear
I sink deeper
in my leather chair
from where I see
the all-consuming
screen.

March 9th
SHE GOT LEGS

I used to strut
my stuff
on heels so high
my legs
twin pegs
I took for granted
in their splendour
are now not
so perfect
curved and bowed
perspective all wrong
and not so long
mottled knees
can barely stand
to wait
for more than five
minutes at a stretch
and yet
I walked this far
along the road
am walking
still.

March 10th
BELOW PAR

a month out
from my birhday
and I'm feeling fine
I will be sixty-nine
soixante-neuf
from a whole new angle
still erect
but not if there's a chair
on which to perch
my sagging rump in soft despair
my chin droops
across my TV screen
I saw it sharpen to a point
amongst the folds
growing old at last
it's exactly what
it's trumped
up to be
no one told it
differently
what will be
will be.

March 11th
GRUMPELSTILTSKIN

repress the grump!
refuse to be
predictable
in discontented rage
at how things change
how dumb they have become
and how they stay
the same
in that time-honoured game
of old

resist the urge
to correct
ignore the disrespect
don't act your age
the way
that they expect
you to
behave

have a nice day?
simply answer
yes
the sun's already set
on that exchange
lose not your temper
in the coffee queue
accept the nuisance
of your name

keep your distance
from the drive
to give advice
be not the baggage who
is such a know-all
with a cranky tone
stereotypical crone
play with your smart phone and
think twice
keep yourself nice!

March 12th
PINK CHAMPAGNE

there will be nightmares
I can feel them
marshalling their steeds
outside my door
and in my veins
nostrils flaring
eyes aflame
too scared to lay my head
upon the pillow
of indulgence

in my cups
I'll just wake up
at three and four and five
scared alive
kick off the covers
mount the stairs
up to the couch
to wait for them
to canter
from my brain
into the magpie dawn.

March 13th
THE URGE

notes from a throat
words on a page
wool on a needle
yarn on a hook
telling a song
writing a book
baking a tart
planting a seed
pruning a rose
playing a part
marrying
burying
naming
declaiming
sewing some clothes
framing a shot
constructing a plot
solving a clue
it's what I do
to get through
to you.

March 14th
MELLO HELLO

I took a step
to bridge the gap
in hope
my move might work
in search of
kindred spirit
that clicked once
before
and might
again
I took the chance
it's all I've got
no hope
to test the worth
of what I made
to make the grade
all on my own
to find the key
to pick the lock
to put the pages
on the block
for all to see
and read
and maybe like
I made the move
to put it right
to find the thread
to lead me from the maze
into the light.

March 15th
THE NATURE OF ART

happy snapping
nature picks
life rushes by
its sweet parade of joy
the cellphone camera eye
is shooting trees
and rainbows
roses
moonglow
sundown kangaroo
cloudland cockatoo
as if
to make them last

it's not enough to stare
to marvel
stand in awe
we have to share
or else
they were not seen at all
the tree in that dense forest
did not fall

our one hand snapping
throws the switch to real
a choice of filter
more appeal
makes us feel
that we can
maybe
trap fog in a jar
catch a falling star and
save it on our desktop
never let it fade
away.

March 16th
I GOT DEM OL' HISTORIC CAVEWOMAN BLUES AGAIN, MAMA

historic bullying
flesh out
current claims
present anarchy
terror reigns

where's the balance?
how to set the frame
before the break
splits atoms into pockets
Korean rockets
and all the world's on edge
memories of Kruschev
and his banging shoe
who knew?
five decades on
we'd be back here again?

Pandora and her box
the gift that keeps on giving
a curse upon the living
but no hope

we spared the rod
the cat's hung out to dry
and mothers sigh
we gave the nod
to children calling shots
or being shot
by clinically insane
grown men
again again again

the world turns
and there's nothing's new
in war-land
no peace, man
'that was just a dream
some of us had'.

March 17th
CHEEK TO CHEEK

old footage
of fleet foot
fancy footwork
white suit
feet
tap-dancing
cross and back
the camera tracking
effortless glide and
bootless charm
no trace
upon the face
of matching song
not going wrong

all gone now
no clue remains
of what you have to do
to hit the heights
of that exquisite skill
no tell-tale stress
upon the dial
of over-sell
of captains barking 2-3-4!
the eyes and teeth
the heads-up front

so casual it seems
walk in the park
to hit the mark
to find the light
to match the band
at beat for beat
no bead of sweat
queers the effect
of what we all might do
if we just knew
our right foot
from our left.

March 18th
CLASSIC

books we read
when we were green
and self-obsessed
and in our teens
force feeding
deadline hitting
target meeting
no spare time
for due attention
to those chapters
strewn before us
like so many pearls

we read to score
to seek the key
to please the don
to prove we knew
stuff
we knew nothing
only now
at days' end
half-forgotten facts
float back
reminders of the works
I thumbed
when I was dumb
and chasing after something else
half-cocked
and full of
me

we come to books
in time
when we are ready
for those big fat tomes
tiny skinny poems
when minds are open
to divine
their meaning-full-ness
line by line.

March 19th
BLOOD RIVER

unlucky street
beside the river
three houses in a row
three mothers who lost sons
one to madness
one to death
and one we'll never know

blood river
boneyard slick runs down
no houses at the brink
the slime creeps up
to number five
but passes number six
on to seven
with the curse
no one home at nine
no matter
it will follow you
to snatch your child
in time

three mothers
and their lovely crop
of sons gone missing
one's never coming back
one's disappeared into the mist
one left his home without a kiss

and tears fall down
towards the river
wombs clench up
with hot remembered pain
that once brought joy
that made a boy
to never see
again.

March 20th
THEY CALL IT HUMPDAY NOW

remember when Wednesday
ceased to signify?
and suddenly
you knew
there'd be another one
next week
a Thursday and a Monday, too
Wednesdays that renewed
like clockwork
lost their school-time
weight
the heft of Monday
joy of Friday
while
you had to wait
for Wednesday
to cross over
names reduced
to heartbeats
ebbs and neaps
the tidal shift
of blood
beneath the skin
Wednesdays
rolling out
and in.

March 21st
EXOTICA NOMADICA

camel saddles and canals
bum-boats, jungles
kilts and bangles
the Bitter Lakes
the open water
Spanish scarves on foreign wharves
seven seas
in ocean liners
heat and dust
and ice and snow
round and round the world
we go

bananas hung in paper bags
snakes in baskets
kids in rags
cottages and Sunday School
platforms 5 and 9 and 2
gully, gully, gully, gully, gully
the Wye valley
and the Rhine
the Rock
the ragged rascal ran
up to the apes
a snowman grinning at my gate

the night-boat
from the Hook of Holland
another bunk
another cabin
hotel breakfasts
German taverns
no toilet in the dog-box
constant pressure
station to station
bony legs crossed
wee fixation
white cliffs of Dover
down the shaft
crumbling barracks
adders hissing in the grass
down the Redoubt and
up the castle
Windermere and windmills
Gurkhas and salt pills
this is my childhood
seen and heard
kaleidoscopic vision
mash-up of the world.

March 22nd
THE BOOK OF FRIENDSHIP

I stuck a book
behind a gate
to mend a wall
of hate
I didn't warrant
(for a change)
I share your pain,
cold woman
I know the wounds
the cuts
the fucked-up misery of it all
and so
I hid a book
for you to find
to change your mind
inside your walled garden
hoping you won't
chuck it in the bin
distrusting everything
the bad old world might bring

a book on birds it is
wild birds you like to feed
you love those fuckers
screeching beaks
wings a-flutter
in the clutter of your seed

I hope you read it
that it brings you joy
it won't bring back
your missing boy
his little wings
have long since flown the coop
have made your shoulders droop
in sorrow's
lonely loop.

March 23rd
ROUND ONE

first round
hearts pound
thrills amongst the swill
of beer cups
and chip trays
hip hip hoorays
fat people
in small seats
leap to their feet
as one
to scream and yell and hiss
a goal, a point, a miss
an umpire doesn't notice
what's in front
of his
dead brainless eyes
blood curdling cries
and threats of violence
rend the clammy air
beneath the gaping roof
where seagulls swoop
like they were at the beach!

it's March too hot for sport
and long walks to the jam-packed train
where claustrophobia
almost wrings the joy
out of the night
what a great fight
what a team
you shoulda seen 'em
in full flight
in red and black
the footy's back!

March 24th
PORT FAIRY SOUTHERN

beach dogs
so very happy
run and run and run and run
and back they come
for more
a ball, a stick
they can't believe their luck
all that sky
all that sand
so much to sniff
to play with
other dogs to arse-check
not for long
they have to run and run and
wait a minute
where's she gone?
she's taking off her clothes
again
she's never going in
to hit the water
she whistles
okay
here we are
we were busy with some wrack
now we're in up to our necks
and it's so wet!
so unpredictable

you go
we'll stay here
rock-high
keep nit
every day the same routine
just when we start
to have some fun
she's in her undies
stroking sideways
and we pace about
in case she drowns
in case of sharks
what would we do?
search me

we are beach dogs
with so much to do
while land-dogs sniff
each other's poo
we are
running, pacing,
tongues out
lashing
two by two.

March 25th
DIMINSHING APOSTLES

getaway
for just a day
(two really)
hit the open road
to stay the night
the miles unfold
in green delight
sightseeing
the familiar and the strange
within range
thoughts rearrange
and jolt the dull routine
sharp winds
from off the ocean
slice through brains
slammed up against a rail
to cop the beauty
of the sea
terrifying coastline
crumbling reality
frightening power
of surf and brine
pulverising
rock to sand
sculpting the land
in stark
inevitability.

March 26th
TO AUTUMN, TOO

and suddenly
we're swathed in wool
a leaf fall
chimes the urgent need for socks
just yesterday
my feet were fat and
bulging
fit to bust
through
heatwave upon heatwave
rolling shut
god's own electric blanket
with the temp dialled up to 3
stifling thought
of anything
but cold and damp and wet and
a stiff breeze
through the hungry curtains

o, blessed April
come at last
fire me
with an arctic blast
in your blessed
month of chill

before the heaters
get switched on
before the fires
blaze in the grate
instead of decimating
bone dry country towns
before we turn
the doona down
a few short weeks
of crisp sharp welcome
coolth
in which to get shit done
without the constant throb
of blood upon the boil
and floods of sweat
and sleepless nights
and pillows wet
before the bite of winter
snaps
I cry out welcome!
Autumn.

March 27th
ROCK VENUS 1

show coming
sold
but not constructed
pin-pricks of fear
stab at my gut
be okay on the day
be alright on the night
and yet and yet
the fright
that queasy feeling
of uncertainty
have I finally
bitten off a bite
too big for me to chew?
it was ever thus
the more we fuss
the better we pull through
tightrope walker
don't look down
that way disappointment lies
upstanding
is the prize.

March 28th
"LEAVE ME ALONE"

words fail me
grief impales me
to a numbness
I become less
than I ever thought I'd be
who could have seen
the way the thing pans out
the infinite cruel variety
of broken heart
I crawl into a tight space
like a box
and I can't find ways
to make it stop
and there's the truth
it's not about what I can do
it's not about what I must learn
to accept
the plot
is not in my hands
it's in his hands
with those long, soft fingers
that I made.

March 29th
SMELL THE SERENITY

'to accept the things
I cannot change'
rise above the strange
embrace the weird
acknowledge the feared
bend to the blow
know how to go
forward
upward
onward
in a straight line
mine the carnage
into gold
reject the chains that bind
rage against the grind

'to accept the things
I cannot change'
find smart ways to behave
cut the losses
weigh anchor
pitch the tosser
banish rancour
calm waters ahead
the past is dead
cue Gloria Gaynor
what she said.

March 30th
CORDELIA

flying home
she is
tomorrow brings
her here
to where she was
before
but not for long
soon gone
and so rejoice
in it
it will be nice
to have her snarky presence
keeping me in line
for a time
my arms extend
towards that happy blend
of generations
my heart will close
around a sweeter place
a fond embrace
perhaps a balm
for my cracked soul.

March 31st
APRIL FOOL

spaghetti trees
the BBC
and chocolate eggs
get hatched by rabbits
jesus rolls away the stone
the coffin cheater
happy easter
up he goes
he's heaven-bound
above the ground
to sit by Dad
and make us glad
that business on the cross
is done
we'll signify it with a bun
in packs of six at Coles
take four days off
and have some fun
reversing hemispheric roles
antipodean rites of spring
down-under autumn
leaves are turning brown
and falling from
spaghetti trees
the shops are open
no one goes to mass
or sings the hymns
in holy keys
such a wheeze
this God-less Easter
heathen trash
pagan Eostre
cold memories
of a sacred past.

april....

April 1st
EASTER LAYING DOWN

my head aches
'and a drowsy numbness'
is sending me all Keats
raw crunch
of pain between the eyes
fear of what's to come
at 3 a.m.
because
come it will
wine swill
and chocolate in bars
and a crucial lack of food
has seen to that
the carnal urge
to lay out flat
despite knowing that will hurt
and heart attacks
crouch in wait beneath the sheets
and, so, to bed
to wake up dead
and swearing
black is white
to never be this way
again.

**April 2nd
TECHNOLOGY**

how will we remember
if it isn't written down
if it isn't printed out
all is ether now
a cloud
of infinite variety
spinning out in twos and ones
endless capacity to capture
thought
word
deed
meal
sea shore
kiss
but not what's real

we are condemned
to the eternal
now
the dream
in which we think
we nailed it
has failed to comprehend that
all is
fog between the fingers

the past disintegrates
in cyber-flash
a glitch
a virus
and it's gone
and we are left
no ancient books
with faded scrawl
no crinkle-cut snaps
upon the wall of time
to remind us
who we were
what we did and said
what we learned
as the old world
turned
to new.

April 3rd
THE MEAT MARKET

it's been my thrill
for just a song
to occupy
old fond buildings in this town
grey palaces of dreams
and schemes and
marbled broken hearts
my current haunt's
a labyrinth of
long cool corridors
unmarked doors
winding toward
my special place
above the hall
where blood flowed free
from racks of lamb
and piggy-wigs
and beef for Irish stew

o, if these walls could speak
the talk would be of chops
and snags
and butcher's hooks
not books
or plays or jazz or fugue
striped aprons
gumboots streaked with gore
thick sawdust clumped upon the floor

now the only knives you'll score
are in the communal kitchen drawer
and artists carve their way
through glass
and words and notes
and tenderise
scenarios and festivals
of sound and light
their noses pressed up tight
against small screens
creating dreams
to feed the mind
and stir the soul

my little room
my refuge and my quiet cell
above the pumping pub
my window shakes
and birds choir in the evening sky
I walk the halls
in gratitude
and dread the day
I'd have to say
goodbye.

April 4th
SCREEN SAVER

Bronte blues
on my home screen
careen my soul
I want to plunge
into your cool green stripes
along the bumpy pool
and feel the spray
sight the vasty
safe beyond the rocks
the spume
the crash
the swell
the fall
I want to crab
down old white steps
and clutch at rails
stained with rust blood
the fundamental
blue and white
it calls to me
with siren ocean song
body thirst
that's what it is
a yearning
for immersion
to ease the shock of life
a longing for the deep wet crystal clear
if I lived close by here
I would get nothing done.

**April 5th
KEEPING HOUSE**

the accusation
glint of steel
beneath the smile
for you have fucked up
with your act of love
your act of care
your act of kindness
not required

it has fucked up
you will pay
and you will pay
and you will pay
for even thinking
you were wanted
needed
you were not.

you should just fuck off
and keep your judgy nose
out of her world
or feel the wrath
of that steely, savage smile
of accusation
and resentment
and of bile

you are a no one
and not needed
never was
don't be the mother
that you had
and loved
she is not needed
wanted
never was.

April 6th
NOT MY BIRTHDAY BUT STILL

a night off the couch
out of the house
on the town
getting down
with the boomers
at a band
on the strand
off the leash
where I belong
on song
where happiness resides
in tune
in light
feels right
top night.

April 7th
TO DONOVAN

'it's Saturday night
feels like a Sunday
in someways'
if I had any sense
I'd maybe go way
for a few days
to sit like Donovan said
'in the valley of Scorpio
beneath the cross of Jade'
when the Leitch
was the man for the mood
I could still sit cross-legged
and stand up in one move
fluted hippy dreams
in melody
Steel-Eye Span
Scott MacKenzie
The Starship
Incredible String Band
and I am flying
in my witch's hat
'wearing black cherries for rings'
to 'rooms that I have lived in'

whitewashed walls
posters of Marx, Marlon, Marilyn
dial-up phone in the hall
my mind fresh and keen
newly ripped from my teens
yearning for communion
of spirit
so young
highly strung
not stoned
slightly alone
with my thoughts
adrift and in focus
in a higher zone.

April 8th
LASAGNE

too fat to write
stuffed as an olive
to excess
shoved down goose gullet
with greedy, grasping claws
spoon against fork
sausage and pork
exploding with cheese I am
engorged with grease I am
chockas with cream I am
my gut pushes out
to 9 months tight
expecting quins I am
bursting at the seams
repeating
up the down staircase
gas and bile bad dreams
first world glutton
can't find the STOP button
lamb chop and mutton
all the fuel that fits
and then more
the consequence
is corpulence
is effluent
is flatulence
and more.

April 9th
LUNCH

doesn't take much
to burst my bubble
vulnerable
gagging for trouble
a word flies wide
across the table
and I am punctured
flat
unable
gone for all money
limp with shame
questioning past words I've said
as bad
named names
they'd've been sinking, too
shrinking from my company
if they knew
choosing to eschew

my horny skin
stretched tight and thin
fears the stealthy random pin
unbidden
poised
to put me in my place
to face disgrace
to shut my face.

April 10th
BRAVO TANGO FOXTROT GOLF

it takes two to tango
so
dance me
to the end of love
around the floor
a-go-go
in perfect time
legs entwined
rhythm with a pattern
and a shape
and some rules
to the moves
neither one of us
to call the shots
but the teacher
with the nous
and the journey
through the time
is on the four
or on the one
it could be fun
we'll never know
until we go
until we come
to the end
of the dance.

April 11th
PANIC STATIONS

knotted gut
stress cancer reflux
every answer bad
messing with my head
thinking dead
thinking path to death
thinking last breath
thinking counting down
thinking thinking thinking

happy birthday, me
last stop to 70
last of the 60s
and I am 18 again
in my narrow single bed
St Teresa in my head
knowledge fresh
of fate
heart rate
up and sloshing
through the pipes
mother down the hall is
no fucking help at all

knotted gut
stomach cut
what a way to go
maybe tomorrow
it will be….. okay.

April 12th
HOLY ICON

rosaries and holy cards
statues of the virgin
infants of Prague
mother of pearl
Christ on a cross
Christ on a bike!
all faith lost
these icons remain
hard to explain
why they clutter my shelves there
mysterious selves
signifying something
god knows what
except he's not around
to thicken the plot
never was
not for me
maybe briefly
statuary remains
flaming hearts in frames
trinkets and chains
holy water bottle
the mind boggles
'tis a puzzle
and a gaudy one
bless me father
for I have
placed false idols before you
in full view.

April 13th
A MIGHTY WIND

the wind is up
flyscreens flutter
leaves disgorge from moss-choked gutters
curtains flap
and shake the shutters
dust swirls gritty in hall corners
up through floorboards
up the smallest cracks
the wind is fresher
branches sough and moan
as if their boughs would break
and bow to pressure

season's changing
snuggletime is rearranging
wool and raincoats
hearty stews
beefy rains, icy dews
footy scarves
heated cars
tights and boots and covered shoes
the winter blues
in swingtime
bring it on

dull heat begone
slate back to me
the comfort of a window shut
a fire blazing in the grate
pruning roses
turning earth
beneath a leaden sky
sighs of relief
summer, goodbye!

April 14th
GONE GIRL 2

quiet now
she's gone
once more
no more
scattered coffee splashes
sopping towels upon the floor
water water everywhere
mugs and glasses strewn
jars unscrewed
sodden laundry
wide back door
flagrant disregard
for safety
or security
she's gone
and all is quiet now on the western front
and all the petty quarrels of last month
fade into obscurity
she is what she is
my peach
my prickly pear
and she is gone
for quite a while
and I will miss her
million dollar smile.

April 15th
AU FROMAGE

if I were a cheese
I'd be aged to perfection
it says so right there
on my birthday card
if I were a cheese
I'd be tough as old Edam
like parmesan I'd be hard
bitey and crumbly
rough round the edges
runny and soft under pressure
and the smell, dear god,
as of rotten vegies
I'd ask for something fresher

if I were a cheese
I'd be goat
bearded and ornery
fearsome and sacred
inscrutable horny
antisatanical
friend of the thorny
no baby bell cheddar
no camp port salut
if I were a cheese
I'd be blue.

April 16th
SERVICE BRAT PACK

service brat
that is my clan
my country
who I am
no homeland
we are gypsy
free range eggs
cuckoo spawn
allegiance to the oddest gang
binds us
like no other
sister brother
raised in different lands
but bound
unto the clan
of service brat
the empire's rag-tag tribe
made by NAAFI BFES BAOR HQ
how to explain
the joy, the pain, the constant new
of fractured childhood
safe and whole
across the sea
across the sand
hand in estranged familiar hand.

April 17th
RECORDS

slices of music
squashed into rows
circles of sound
flattened rounds
of flattened fifths
funky riffs
ground into grooves
chapters of taste
hit parade waste
three decades wide
finite collection
pop jazz and classical
folk soul and comical
section to section
alphabetical order
Zappa to Animals
Aretha to Wonder
vulnerable pliable
handled with care
'til CDs took the lead
superseded
all air now
cybersonic
all files

but my miles of LPs
in the shelves of the lounge
are old friends
objets d'art
catch at the heart
at the sight of a sleeve
scratch and crackle
of diamond on vinyl
slide cross side A to side B
take time to flip over
not forgetting to blow
fluff from the needle
lay back and remember
the first time you spun it
where you were
what you felt
how you read every word
every lyric
every clue to the mind
of the idol who made it

slices of music
fragments of memory
pressed close together
or leaning apart
music as art.

April 18th
HOPE SPRINGS

hope is a tiny flame
that flickers in the slightest breeze
and so I keep
my hands wrapped tight
around my heart
to keep the draught of failure out
and hold my breath
and calm my pulse
and dare to dream
that I might hold the fort
enough
to live to see it through
this little seed of mine
into a tree
divine.

April 19th
ROCK RÔLE

blowing cobwebs off the larynx
hear them go
welcome back rock 'n roll
my love for you
has not decreased
I heart you
with each crashing beat
each jangling chord
and throbbing bass
in your face
in the moment
in the groove
room to move
my old familiar stomp
that sweet familiar pace
no time for clever
points to score
nothing to prove
four on the floor
rock the room
ba-boom!
if they let me
stand my ground
I'll stay upright, on mic
until I'm found de trop
and can't cut the show
but for now
I'm back where I belong
on song.

April 20th
GLUTTONY

fully sick
panic constricts
my gullet
'must've been that sandwich I ate"
could've been that bottle I scarfed
like water
oughta think twice
before pouring out thrice
the limit
grateful it wasn't the full Aristotle
flushed down my gorge
with the omelette
chillee sauce
and the sarni grilled
cheese, of course
lashings of full fat
and pickles
fully sick I'll
be sorry
tomorry.

April 21st
HUM-A-BUZZ-BUZZ

a bumblebee rests on my neck
tiny golden charm
attracts the eye of passers-by
like bees to flowers
pollen hunting
chick-magnet is my bee why?
I fell for it, too
had to have it round my neck
sought it on the internet
until that bee was mine and dusted
bargain-priced
gold-encrusted
messengers from underworld
from us and back they say
bees understand us
sense our thoughts
try to teach us
more sweet skills
than honeycomb production
wisely buzzing
chain reaction
butterfly effect
civilization as we know it
depends upon the bee
one stung me one time on the knee
in my grandpa's allotment
it meant a lot to me
now, there's this bee
suspended round my neck.

April 22nd
FREE PARKING

carpark manners oxymoron
we are tigers prowling
stalking spaces
we are panthers, pumas
pacing
in the deadly chase
scanning faces
trailing trolleys with intent
second guessing
where and how long to the car
which direction and how far
feral we are
alley-cat jumping
tyre squeal, horn blast
hearts a-thumping

I saw it first!
Oi! you dickhead
that's my indicator blinking
it was flashing way before
yours came on
don't make me open up this door
don't make me swing the baseball bat
that I have hidden in my boot
knuckles dragging on the floor

I have to buy some peas!
please!
don't make me shoot you
there's a special in JBs!
don't make me smash your teeth in
just give in
drive on from this spot
and suck it up.

I feel so smug
I've scooped a bay
whip my phone out
brake lights on
to play awhile on twitter
Facebook Instagram
a thug approaching
gun held high
threatening some other guy
dumb enough
to back in when he should've gone in straight!
time to meet your fate, mate
in this game of thrones
hatchback kings
concrete jungle
the monkey swings
musn't grumble.

April 23rd
DE FACTO

to reach the point
where nothing's said
companionship is dead
radio silence
on what matters
the shallow barb
the hollow chatter
the two steps back
anti-natter
if we could banter
like we do outdoors
what fun we'd have
we'd be set for life
in this palace of yours
in these spacious rooms
how I long to smash the glass
cry havoc
loose the dogs of truth
confront the ghastly spectre
of our ruined love
of your wasted years
of my stifled tears
how I long to set you free
to love
to fuck
to simply be
yourself
as you would love
to be.

April 24th
WHAT IS IT GOOD FOR

the family trade was warfare
generations long
the king's shilling
empire men
that was us
on both sides of the blanket
waging conflict far and near
captain major grenadier
uniformed formation
fall in line
follow orders double-time

not for us the call to arms
the noble cause
the one-off save the nation
business-as-usual
steady trade
useful occupation
that was our vocation

unscathed children
long to feel
what their forefathers felt
the blood
the rot
the open wound
the mateship
in the tent

virtual reality installations
welcome you to battle stations
whine of bullet
flash of bomb
wade through mud
just like the Somme
except it's not.

why would you want that?
your long dead forebears
wouldn't wish it on a dog
fetishism pure and simple
tourist dollar
tweets and blogs

I respect the sacrifice
each truck of cannon-fodder made
to help their rulers
play at chequers
lobbing human hand grenades
but being in the family trade
I feel no urgent need to parade
or celebrate
some theme-park war
as if we lived in peace

you wanna visit battlefields?
and graveyard acres?
take your pick
there's wars a-raging as we speak
embrace the lucky
shun the crass
it isn't Moomba
the simple past.

April 25th
ARTHUR

my left leg walks in perfect time
no pains no aches no quirks
my right leg is aged ninety-nine
it creaks it jars it shirks
from walking
standing
climbing stairs
it prefers to sit in chairs
wherever it can find them

at the apex of these legs
the barely aged
the crippled peg
I try to strike a balance
but my camber is off-key
between the way
one leg should stand
and grim reality.

April 26th
PERIOD

tracking the blood
month by month
new moon full moon
28 days
marking due dates
danger zones
the ebb the flow
the tide of life
the circled P
that called the tune
that made the rules

the time to clean
the moody days
the time for sex
the bad hair phase
(never cut or colour when the P is marked)
life to order
a regulated plan
a shape a structure
not this bland
unchanging evermore
'til death

fertility tracked upon a grid
acute awareness of the possibility
of kid
of getting rid
of what you did
in case you did
ignore
the trail of blood
the pulse and throb
of life
marked out in lunar cycles
punctuated
with a
P.

April 27th
No.64 BEFORE COMPLETION

very i-ching, Homer
in my end
is my beginning
I used to throw
those three brass coins
and ask important questions
in my head
never said out loud
facing north
upon my solo bed
oracle swathed in purple silk
replied
in sixes, sevens, eights and nines
called my fate
in images so vague and strange
I'd stare and stare
words upon a page
composed in China
in a different age
                alien culture
                ordered state
and yet
I'd find a way to make them
resonate
in my green and Fitzroy modern life
of unrequited love
and stalled ambition
seeking wisdom
thrown by
permutations
combinations
explanations
of the incomprehensible
the human condition.

April 28th
SKIN DEEP

Helen Mirren wakes
to face the mirror
moonscape over solid structure
hair askew perhaps
eyes not quite clear
but true
grey enough
to stare down one more day of challenge
purpose strong
a long life filled
with intent
not content to settle
I would Helen Mirren be.

I awake
to curse the night before
shun the mirror
hide and run
chinless now
thinning hair in ragged patches
shiny scalp
a bulging paunchy not so raunchy
sagging beanbag of a woman
no one loves much
a long life filled
with regret
discontent
I would settle
for an undisclosed sum.

April 29th
ARIELS

it's mermaids for me
not unicorns
as myths go
the comb the mirror
seaweed tresses
cheeky breasties
just enough to send salts mad
the fishy tail the flashing smile
rainbow scale beneath the foam
the now-you-see-me-now-you-don't game
of catch me if you can
you dumb forked humans
on the sand

that unicorn horn
looks like a headache and
when all is said and done
it's just a horse
a Scottish nag, at that
no eerie singing, no discourse
just ghosting woodlands
free of sin
with only a virgin to lay
a hand upon milky skin
to reel him in
and then what?
porn?
o, give me a home 'neath a rolling bay
and a mermaid any day.

April 30th
COLD

little germs
stay away
don't fuck with me
today
I don't need you in the mix
I don't want your tiny pricks
perforating confidence
and hope
I only want the good guys
of your team
in my stream of life
lacto bacto Cilla Black
gimme that stuff
in my ileac
digestive tract
but not the ones
that scratch the eyes and throat
and rip the lining from the nose
I don't want those
take two steps back
or I will nuke you with big drugs
you nasty
soul-destroying
thugs.

may....

May Day
WAKE IN FRIGHT

can you die of a broken heart?
the papers say you can
they've done a scan
monitoring pain
right up to the tipping point
of death
last breath
'why didn't you love me?'
Jean Paul Belmondo lies bleeding
in the dirt
could not take the hurt
any more than I can
they've done a scan
tracked poison oozing out of hearts
into the dark
and blackest regions of the soul
conducted polls
surveyed the inner zones
iced bitter cold
snap-frozen from a lack of warmth
of pity tender nurture
they've grown a culture
tossed it to a vulture
who declined
they've yet to find a cure

love comes too late
to save you
from what's lacking
the damage done
the forked tongue
the acid flung
what's that squishy sound?
that's one heart
cracking.

May 2nd
WIGGY

today I bought a toupee
hip hooray
a vain attempt
to hide the baldness
hide the fear
beneath a fright wig
because I might freak
if people see my shiny scalp
and whisper
meanness
like I would
if I should spot the same
on some other woman's head

I could wear a scarf
I know
fend off laughs like that
a hat
a turban
that's a fact
I know
but for the mo
(no pun intended)
it's a rug with clips
and fingers crossed
it does the trick.

May 3rd
HORSE AND CARRIAGE

love
is universal now
the sacred vows
the solemn words
the shiny rings
the bows and things
are shared by everyone
not love,
of course,
but formal recognition of
the common urge
that drives us all
to woo
to mate
to procreate
to nest
to cling
cohabitate
until the end of time
with The One
the chosen human fate
has thrown into our path
to share a laugh
a photograph
a dinner here
a concert there
a meal a match
a trip to France

and suddenly you're hitched
like some old Frank Sinatra song
and curled up on the couch of dreams
and making plans
a poodle at your feet

boy and girl
chap and man
girl and gal
and all the other lovers
who can
shack up for the stretch
and make it legal now
'cos that's how
simple
true love is.

May 4th
SPITTING

ducking the rain
nice weather for drakes
we used to complain
about the wet
now we takes what we can get
a fortnight of soaking
a month of damp
unheard of in these sere El Niño days
set the dial to shower
run to catch the bus
the crush
the musty reek of
sodden wool and
squelching boots
coats dripping to a pool
of glorious heaven's tears

three cheers for rain!
(on Jane from Spain)
long overdue
forgotten what to do
when it breaks from the sky
they're running like the water's fire
they only know the dry
don't know why
or what to do
with pitter patter
splish splash I was taking a bath
in the rain.

May 5th
CHICKENFEED

two hard-boiled eggs
scrunch of salt and pepper
in a paper scrap
the perfect snack
no mess no fuss
doesn't even streak the lippy
scarfed in a jiffy
with a satisfying bite
of lovely yellow yoke
and fleshy white
two or three mouthfuls
and it's done
more filling than
two bags of crisps
more tidy than
an apple
or a currant bun
I lick my lips
and crack on with the show
egg-powered
googied
good to go.

May 6th
GRATITUDE AGENDA

tasks of life
when balance between
scream
and exaltation's
whisper thin
when the need to thank
the universe
for three small things
caves in
upon itself
and dissolves within an ocean
of despair
time to put away the pen
and repair
unto the comfort of one's den.

May 7th
'IN'

flowers on the bench
fruit in a bowl
and we are home
we are whole
things in place
a lovely space
to think to dream
relax and scheme
take pleasure
in simplicity
tea with milk
dishes in sink
smeared with stink
of late delicious meals
bellies full
still making room for chocolate
fire in the grate
a comfy bed awaits

flowers on the bench
flags of domesticity and care
a stylish air
of calm and order
light through glass
sun through water
stems and leaves
to bring the outside in
a living thing
says we are
in.

May 8th
QUEEN VICTORIA

no place for jokes
in the hard world of books
but what if your so-called
'voice'
is funny?
not on the money, love
write what you know, they say
that's the go
but not if there's gags
well, not from old bags
who don't know shit about humour
leave the quips to the pros
write sensible prose
that'll get you printed
that'll get you on book shows
talking to those in the know
about serious books
about great Big Ideas
spill out all your secrets
okay, make some up
but not if they're funny
and definitely not
if you have a vulva
write vulgar
morbid obtuse
don't try to be cute
no excuse now
we are not
amused.

May 9th
LOVE IN THE AIR

distant thunder
heartbreaks rolling in
love is paper thin
and fragile
agile
vulnerable
the flame of passion
burnt it out
the bubble fears the pin
stretched taut and full of joy
they're letting go the string
and it is rising
clearing treetops
mountains lakes
into the chilly skies
of unwelcome freedom
and they are single
once again
not paired
the glue unstuck
the fire burned cold
and all is as it was
but for the striking
memory
of the match.

May 10th
THE STARS

daily habit
star check
why?
the sky doth not our cruise control
the planets spin
the seasons roll
moonrise sunset and eclipse
the earth turns
and stargazers ply their trade
in faith
in hope
but not for charity
a daily fee
I stupidly pay gladly
I've gone without before
and
full of doubt
of missing out
on some important sign
some clue
a timeline to prosperity
a lifeline to serenity
daily habit
like a prayer
wresting order
from thin air.

May 11th
MEDICATION

drawers full of pills
drugs to kill
the aches
the twinges
creaking hinges
alcohol binges
gravity's irresistible attraction
contraction of sinew
muscular spasm
not orgasm
the constant need to fight the flames
of everyday pedestrian pains

chin up, girl
crack hardy
no complaints
you ain't hooked up
to life support
just yet.

May 12th
MYERS DAY

Mothers' Day looms
the gloom
a million chrysanthemum blooms
stand wetly in their buckets
cellophane wrapped
celebration of the womb
my mother didn't buy it
plot by Myers
to make money honey
what she said
no tea and toast in bed
for Mummy
we weren't raised with it
she called it shit
and I am her own girl
up to a point

I'd take that breakfast
on a tray
I'd say
first Sunday in May
let me lay in bed 'til nine
that would make my day
hip hip hooray

and now they're grown
and gone
I long for burnt toast
and cold tea
the whole catastrophe
spilled over me
long to hold them
close to me
and bless the day
they learned to call me Mum

the hollow crown
this motherhood
is made of thorns
and bitter sweet
and yet
I bless the day
that they were born.

May 13th
ART

ideas erupt
like bubbles in champagne
constantly fizzing
buzzing like flies
in your head
in your brain
out they pop
in they fly
from the sky
from the sea
from the road
from a key
in the air
in your hair
over there, look and see
in the wind
in a tree

the trick is to catch one
to tame it
to shape it
give structure and form
see it through to the end
do the work
take the time
give it care and attention
make no exception
for sloth or for shoddy
examine the body
of each new creation
adjust to perfection
until close inspection
yields nothing
but joy
in the idea
of something
from nothing
confusion
made clear.

May 14th
THE AUTUMN LEAVES

the moon wanes
stomach pains
hair thins
winter rains
renewal is at hand
leaves like jewels
fall ruby, golden, ash and tan
burnished drifts
curl up beneath the summer table
like abandoned dogs
hard by stacks of fresh hewn logs
exposed to sudden hail

the moon wanes
a scratch of silver
sends a shiver
at the prospect of what's new
what's yet to do
the boogaloo
the hustle and the twist
all grist to the remorseless mill
of cycles in the sky
the sweet by and by.

May 15th
OLD AGE ADAGE

the giftee gee me a gift
and said
this is the back
of your balding head
this is the side
of your spotted face
here is your bosom
where is your waist?
as wide as a cow
don't know how you think
you will cut it now
on stage under lights
a fright to behold
you're too old
for the game
stop kidding yourself
old dame
face the facts get a grip
there's a reason
the good ones last long
stay on song
they put in the work
get work done
do botox keep fit
whatever it takes
to have skin in the game
you've had a good run
had some fun
can't complain.

May 16th
SPITTLE

spit
in the DNA test tube
what to prove
who I am
who my tribe
microbe analysis
searching for clues
in a gob
the point of it is to know
who made me
grow
where they're from
what they
know
where I belong

o, not that again!
never know for sure
what shore
I hailed from
a dribble of spit
might grease the door open
a crack
illuminate the track
winding back
to the line
of heritage
another page.

May 17th
COUNTDOWN

they are dropping like flies
my friends, foes
my peers, pariahs
heroines, heroes
the game of eenie meanie
in full swing
spin the bottle
with a twist
no kiss
but of death
Facebook farewells
tweeted tributes
outrage and dismay
chickens of misspent youth
fly home to roost
ashtrays and empties
swept aside
for the mask, the drip
th'assisted suicide
not him not her
not fair
too soon too soon
mortality's a bitch
unless she's on your side
and you haven't made a will
just yet.

May 18th
SINGING

the voice swells up
feels right
vibrates and soars
to join another
sister brother tone
sweet harmony
joyful awesome
twosome foursome
on the off-beat
can't get enough of
in the zone

songs as comfortable
as trackie dacks
familiar tracks
like blood and nerve and sinew
etched upon my brain
down memory lane
and yet not old
solid gold they are
and I don't care who knows it
and I am in the groove
of easeful repetition
warbling to my heart's content
until the final crotchet.

May 19th
LA MAMA

a building burns
history goes up in smoke
like Alexander's library
a rebuild will not bring it back
it's good bye to that
those walls with ears
each brick an eyeline
each floorboard
some remembered crack
penned by a hack
new minted way back then
squeal of dimmer
churn of urn
a log falls
in the chimney of before
layers of paint on the floor
the time we covered it in sand
played in a band
writhed naked to The Doors
rode a chopper to the door
huddled in darkness on the stairs
sang through the banister
balanced on chairs
made love in a double bed
inches away from the fray
first show-business pay

out out brief candle
of remembered play
life's but a walking shadow
thrown by a random blaze

small building
tiny space
immense consequence
staged its own cremation
utter devastation.

May 20th
PIX

pictures everywhere
the people's art
a scarf a chair
a rose a teapot
smile upon your face
sunflower dog
the space between
a building and a lane
summer rain
a misspelt sign
we take the time now
mark the spot
that moment
we said 'look at that'
we don't have to wait
for chemicals
and special lights
to interpret
what we felt
we touch the app
upload share
filter from thin air
the everywhere.

May 21st
26

the hour of your birth
approaches
reproaches
and all is horror
terror
torture
the walls drip blood
cry 'Atreus!'
unnatural state
our fate is to endure
eternal censure
from our beloved child.

each year is worse
you have cursed us
with your selfish hate
your adolescent hissy-fit
condemns us to this state
of misery
and rage
and blunt incomprehension.

wading through
the birthday hours
without a touch
without connection
to affection
or redemption

grinding gears ungreased
mired in stagnation
of self-hating
lonely self

no absolution
no correction
to this state of
hell.

May 22nd
BIRTHDAY BLUES

and we are through it
home safe
put to bed
tears shed
another anniversary
safely shelved
another grim reminder
of what's lost
the cost so crippling
the effect so stifling
'when harm is done
no love can be won'
the fist clenched round the heart
is cold blue steel
you cannot feel a thing
yet feel it all

now midnight's here
so, raise a cheer
we can relax
and hope for better times
next year.

May 23rd
BURWOOD 1

mother in the lounge
Fler chair orange
relax lay back
fire in the grate
orange red black orange
Not Only But Also, Mavis in a hat
everything is funny in black
and white

darling
have an Irish Mist
have a Drambuie
hold it on your tongue now
inhale don't sip
life lessons late at night
stay
keep me company
sit
in Daddy's chair
no, she never said that
but the lonely was there
me, too, in my way
what a pair
stifled sophistication
Hollywood dreams
suburban scandal-puss with her
leopard-skin schemes

who did she see
when she looked at me?
daughter, friend, sister,
partner in crime
we laughed to sobs
most of the time
Leaping Nuns of Norwich
Pete and Dud
Hancock, Guerney Slade
jazz and cocktails
twelve o'clock tales

mother in the lounge
until the fall of midnight snow
goodnight viewers
cheerio
what I'd give for one more hour
just to know.

May 24th
BURWOOD 2

father in the lounge
leg crooked up on one knee
cup of tea
four sugars more
pile of biscuits
sliced Genoa
brown apple core
ashtray ashtray ashtray ashtray
crossword puzzle frown
dog at his feet
Brylcream crown
glimpsed through thick fog
of 4 o'clock smoke
spade and hoe in the rack
garden hose rolled back
roses fed and watered
stroke the pussy
cheer the Cats
no time for chit-chat
what to say to all those girls?
happiest with the men
at the front
at the mess
at the lodge
in the ring
in the khaki world
of action and endeavour
and orders from the major
by the left quick march

father in the lounge
his castle and his solace
measured rest
R and R
shotgun in the cellar
rods and tackle in the case
and books by the dozen
and ciggies by the carton
and work work work
and cough cough cough

father in the chair
orange chair
in thin air
thick smoke everywhere
never where
I hoped he'd be
in 1970.

May 25th
FREEDOM SONG

I took a walk beside a lake
and the sun
was not yet done
at almost ten
and the sky was tender pink
and grey
still day
soft green leaves
lush green lawn
vole and faun
and all was hushed and gentle
in the pearly northern light.

at water's edge
perched on a ledge
I sang to fish
and swans
old James Brown songs
Gravity, the big G
I was free
it was me
like I used to be
in school day parks
on the swings and monkey bars
playing on my own
until the dark.

May 26th
PINS*

here comes the pain again
jamming up my legs
and defying motion
running skipping jumping
but a memory
bone on bone
gonna finish me
skewered knees
muscles on the twitch
at the slightest hitch
the merest stretch
the reach and fetch
too scared to lie in bed
afraid to rise on pins of lead

no more climbing trees
squatting to pee
no more ladders
must say please
move that picture hang that pot
a walk along the beach is fraught
cobblestones my foot gets caught
rick my joints
no point whingeing
you are trapped
you are too fat
you can change that.

---

*with apologies to The Eurythmics

May 27th
MOONBOOT

little girl in the world
with your foot
in a moon boot
don't mess with the mahout
he won't get you
he'll get at you
with all your trust
and all your wonder
and wide-eye, world-love
empathy
don't labour under any
misapprehension
he is not your friend
he is not your ally
not even if he says so

a mother frets
no matter how many times
little girl in the world
visits hostile climes
gets no easier
to let go
open up the playpen gate
have some faith
little girl in the world will know
all there is to know
moonboot or no.

May 28th
NASTURTIUMS

first seed I stuck in soil
I was a child
somewhere
who knows where
in the world
a little girl
rain falling
perfect
that I know
umbrella high above the squelch
perfect bed
to lay the baby in
nasturtium seed it was
(I had to check the spelling)
I did the same today
and there I was again
a little kid
life's mystery pinched
between thumb and finger
dried nasturtium pea
you don't forget
those lessons someone taught
who was it took the time
to show me what to do?
mother father uncle aunt
hired servant, that'll do

I see a window and a patch of mud
I see the seed and feel it
dry and hard
and know that it will bud
of that I'm sure
the certainty of propagation
is etched in happy affirmation
of life
of flowers
of seasons
hot and cold
young and old.

May 29th
THE SLOUGH

the sulk
it has to be allowed
the right to say
please go away
fuck off and leave me be
to dig my misery
to stew
to brood
indulge my mood
I do not want your sympathy
down to the bottom of the glass
you cannot stop me
do not even try
no hugging please
or I might cry
big fat salt tears into my wine
my concrete face
should be a sign
for you to take a hike
be on your bike
with your don't be such a sissy
and your it'll be all right
I don't want to fight
let me enjoy my hissy
I want to call it quits
embrace the shits
descend into the pits
of leaden bleak poor me
defeat, surrender is a tonic
it feels like winning
against pollyanna smiling odds
and regimented grinning.

May 30th
PAST IMPERFECT

an old lover
his face
looms without warning
and you're back in that place
where you fell
for a spell
should've stayed
on reflection
good times
affection
and sex
but
the big but
butts in
it wasn't him you wanted
really wanted
ate your heart out for
always yearned for more
for the romance
the impossible
attached and
uninterested in you
and you knew it
never happy with
perfect
compatible
flattering
good match

an old lover
his face reappears
and all becomes clear
paths you took
when you shoulda known better
choices you made
when you dreamed you would get a
good man
an angel
to make you happy
against impossible odds

an old lover
his face
rises up out of nowhere
and you feel it
a jolt
electric
as it was.

May 31st
ROCK CHOOK

so grateful
for another run
another crack
at band
at camaraderie
creativity
in music
with a crew
to talk about the show
which way to go
which rock to roll

I took the plunge
I made the call
rise or fall
and we are on our way
a chance to play
another day another night
I've missed that took-for-granted feat
of standing at the mic
in light
with foldback at my feet.

june.....

June 1st
IN A BLUE FUNK

they paint walls blue
whole cities even
and pink and green
and primrose, too
the palate of the world
is wide
not mandated classified
regulated
except here where we live
in green and brownsville
with maroon stripe
dull as national green and gold
what fool decided
Batman's acquisition
should be quite so drear
Boring Road and Same Old Street
row on tedious row
in every shade from beige to taupe
here in Mission Brown Town

and then we see the travel snaps
beamed back from far across the sea
see the bright fantastic world
of colour
avenues of turquoise
high rise flats of scarlet
burnt sienna flecked with green

we can't believe the freedom
other cities have
to make a rainbow
of their streets
reflect the landscape
banish drab

I don't want cartoons
on my wall
or bubble-written
infant scrawl
I want buildings to be vibrant
want the houses to be art.

June 2nd
TO BREAKFAST

tea and toast renewal
breakfast absolution
for last night's transgressions
panadol penance
licence to face another day
of slog
self-driven, wages free

twice boiled water
will not do
gas flame kettle, too
proper bread sawn
with a jagged blade
the table laid
milk-jug, cup and saucer
and, of course, an
iPad page of Age

pink china pot thrice-turned
not urned
fat black leaves eke forth their stain
to drain out from a golden spout
through knitted cosie hole
brown tea
lightly milked unsugared
toast browned
on setting 3
is buttered thickly now
and vegemited to the crusts
salt crunchy bliss
best meal of the day
flushing evil wine away
reassuringly
comfortingly
satisfyingly
okay.

June 3rd
EUROPEAN SUMMER

look at me!
in gay Paree
and me again
on Galway Bay
I'm in a desert
on a ferry
it's boiling here in old New Delhi
I'm eating wild exotic food
I'm going to church
I'm in the Louvre
check me out in Barcelona
I saw the pope!
went to MOMA
caught the tube
rode the Metro
the BART, the LUAS
the bullet train
I've been away
I should explain
but now I'm back
it's like I never left at all
the mirror on my wall
reminds me
I'm the same old me
but poorer
aching with a pressing need
to do it all
again.

June 4th
MOLLY-ROSE QUEEN OF THE DESERT

little girl on a camel
emerald scarf
flying high
eyes bright
arms wide
heart fills with pride

little jewel
in the sand
harsh foreign land
asleep beneath stars
you're amazing
yes, you are.

June 5th
HOMETOWN

thrum of hearth
whirr of dishwasher
strike sweet nocturnal harmony
all is well in hometown
dishes sorted
glass recycled
compost binned
stovetop wiped
floor swept
and all before the midnight hour
there will be no midnight callers
spilling through the trusting hippie door
no roar of 'where's the party?'
no nitrous oxide cylinders
strewn about the floor
no part-time lovers
skulking in from earlier trysts
to win you back with one long kiss
no 'can he stay?' notes
from women with a prior claim
no free-love gropes
no jail-birds looking for a place to crash
no Lebanese hash
no missing cash
no Special K (the cereal kind) stashed
in hope beneath my bed
no messing with my head

yes, all is quiet in hometown
that was long ago
when I was young and fearless
always on the go
knew all there was to know
took no shit
gave no inch
and loved to be alone
as I am now
up late
and in my peaceful home
plates in the rack
garbage out
a pencil in my grasp.

June 6th
THAT'$ WHAT I WANT

solvency
however brief
is luxury
ability to gas the tank
to stay the bank
meet the rent
      the lease
      the phone
make a dent in debt
      for just a mo
a chance to breathe
and not lose sleep
not wake up sweating blood
not do the pre-dawn creep

it will not last
but while it does
I'll try to cast
my bread upon the water
live like I oughta
not spend like flour through sieve

but, o, the sweet relief
of several weeks reprieve.

June 7th
INTREPID BLONDE

Albrecht the hare
is in my life
for better or for worse
mystic penpal
golden presence
random contact
across the universe
I don't quite get yet
but somehow embrace
the whiff of strange
exotic brain
quixotic strain

down the hare hole
off I go
how many emails will he send
how will it end
I don't really care
Albrecht the hare
don't need to know
how it will go
the spooky universe
messaging me
cyber synchronicity.

June 8th
OLD FRIENDS

little heart
beating still
against the odds
against the swill
of just so much dislike
the spike of venom loaded
during pleasantries
over cheese
the mood goaded
to the point of hurt
the point at which
you realise the misery
you create
by simply being alive
how do you survive
the tide of phlegm
and wake each day
to know that
you are shit?

June 9th
HOOT!

an owl in our tree
never hungry
possums galore
gnarly bats to gnaw
but how to score one
how to lure a beaky sentinel
to the cypress in the dell
should we carve a box
hang a sign saying WOL
contact Christopher Robin
summon Pooh and Piglet, too

O, an owl would do
the job so well
and our tree is going begging
how splendid it would be
to see a pair of big round eyes
looming
perched
in the branches
of our tree.

**June 10th
ACTION**

making space
changing space
a place to breathe
a little freer
raise the bar
roll away the stone
part curtains
open hearts and windows
new ideas replace the worn
familiar paths don't make for home

take action, stodge!
remember how you moved
to your own tune
without fear
now you dodge and cringe
deny your own idea
within a set routine
small changes
rearrangements
can be the very key
to make for free.

June 11th
TABLETS

tv tv tv tv
Netflix SBS and Stan
tv tv tv tv tv
I am stumped on a divan
murder murder war and gore
death and sex and not much more
I'm glued to it
can't look away
addicted to the max
violence violence and intrigue
candles dripping wax
crusted velvet
nylon backpack
gun and rope and knife
creepy men with cruel intentions
so unlike real life
not a seedy family member
uncle auntie husband wife
no twisted relative in sight
all are strangers
hidden dangers
lurking in the night

plots begin to interlock
can't remember who is what
I just lie there in a knot
clicking buttons
freezing muting skipping ads
guzzling skads
of wine and chocolate
going quietly mad

tv tv tv tv
this is what my life is now
mobile iPad laptop too
it's all screens and
thrills and screams
they have got me
in their zoo.

June 12th
EXES

seismic shift
the past revealed to be
just that
gone
kaput
consigned to history
no going back
be not afraid to chuck
to jettison the truckful
of remembered times
when stars were in your eyes

paths diverge
and re-emerge on different sides
of distant hills
visible
unreachable
not worth fighting through
the undergrowth
to find them
lost
unrecognisable
going nowhere
well,
not with you.

**June 13th
ON TOUR**

anonymous rooms
beige carpet
familiar as life's work
my office
my happy place
a door, a key
facilities
glasses in paper bags
irrelevant mags
sheets the wrong way out
silence
and the TV
remote
space and time
mine
and free
containing me
at work
at what I do
plus the view
another new
familiar
strange
old town.

**June 14th
ON TOUR 2**

pizza at night
musicians' delight
ENOs at dawning
musicians' warning
cram salt at your peril
at close of P.A.
crisps, olives, brie
stick fast for a day
no flushing away
with mini-bar water
wine lines the walls
of your shrinking aorta

sound-check was boring
the gig was okay
no time to eat
the old pay to play
hand me that bottle
that bucket of snacks
it all tastes so good
let's just relax
a pizza? yeah, great
line 'em up, order two
old hacks never learn
they just do the do.

June 16th
OLD ROPE

empty workhouse
where men toiled
in misery
in happy industry
companionship and pay
beer at close of day
camaraderie
tools of tradie
all gone
to clean
expensive bloodless
switch and wire
modus operandi
in the sky and not a
human hand in sight
remembered laughs and dramas
ringing out
in ghostly waves
throughout these cold abandoned and
sepulchral caves
to fall on
rainwashed concrete floors
roofless, bootless
nevermore to hack
the steel-cap tread
those days are dead
here where the air
choked thick with smoke
and dirt and gas
and flying sparks
and welded arcs
of making stuff

the working man and woman
the floorsweeper
and the tearoom crew
pressed hard
around the urn and fag
all gone now
what's man/woman to do?
them that made things
good things
strong and true
to last until their time was through
and longer
the workhouse closed now
walls are smashed
bulldozers charging up and back
relentess
in pursuit of new
to fracture lives
erect an anthill
where once there was
a hive.

June 17th
A NEW KIND OF WET PATCH

little squirts of wee
bursting free of me
leave damp reminders
of bleak reality
warnings
of senility
when they will laugh at me
behind their hands
pads and bags
wrinkled hags
slumped in misery
parked round TVs
have their beady eyes
on me
waiting for a cup of tea
to make more
wee.

June 18th
BALLS

the round ball and the oval
the slender and the thick
the neck the thigh
men flying high
or prancing mudless on a pitch

the round ball, Irish dancing
oval, the Olympics
round ball fans all balls galore
dull moaning the same songs
the oval's tribes have dicks and tits
men women, old and young

the game of life
played out on fields
where drops of blood
must not be shed
and young men lay in bed
at night
and live to fight
another day.

June 19th
FELLOWSHIP

we who work art's saltmines
with no reason
than we must
are always bust
and trust too much
that everything will be okay
the shits will pay
it's not the why, the end
it is the how will we endure
to eat to rent to drive to drink
to create more and more
stuff no one really wants
until they see it
for themselves
so, we must nurture
fellow slaves
when all the odds
are stacked against
recognise, reward, applaud
the song the picture
tread of boards
the story, poem
speech or act
and when we can, back up
with cash.

June 20th
MOONGLOW

a Maxfield Parrish sky
he wrote the book on blue
or mixed the paint
the perfect tint
to catch the close of day
last rays
of washed-out winter sun
when tiny stars
come out to play
on his matte flat canvas
blue dies down
to yellow
far below
and we can dream
of nymphs on rocks
in moonglow
in ravines
in crazy scenes
with pierrots, peacocks
wizards, Grecian urns
Nordic sirens
roaming lost
in pink and purple trees
a world of legend
that endures
and rears its head
through my North Melbourne windscreen
homeward bound.

June 21st
MILITARY BYE-BYE

last post and poppies
a long life and glad
the national flag
the ode
the bugle
and the promise to remember
and to honour
and be grateful
for a proper span
born of survival
and an endless lust
for life
a twinkle in the eye
that did not die
without a wife
the forward thrust
against the dust
and a ready laugh
your epitaph
was
don't you make a fuss.

June 22nd
SPITTLE 2

the DNA
is here
to stay
to stain
mortal remains
the recipe
the formula
the make-up
of the cellular CV
what made me
me
the shamrock and the rose
Thor's hammer and the Rarebit
and a tiny brush of tar
that's what I are
what came down to me
from ancestry (the website)
in a conga-line of letters
jiving through the decades
to their own peculiar tune
the one that croons my name
proclaims my state
my Jane-ness
definitive
immemorial
incarnate.

June 23rd
CAREFUL, THEY MIGHT HEAR YOU

silence
it's the best option now
better not trip over your
tongue
shut up
about China
about gender
about cultural distinctions
facing extinction
subjugation to the undistinguished bland
shut up
about safety
variety
propriety
imperialism past
and the oh-so-frightening present
silent
as the flow of money
through the internet

watchdogs crouch
in cyber corners
armed to the tweet
ready for the glitch
a whiff of bitch
a chance to snitch
at your expense

to pull the holier-than-thou card
but not so holy
not allowed
not out loud
except to sanction
every code
every way to say
it's still okay
to shut a woman's trap
because a HE said so
long ago
centuries back

silence
it's the best option now
even for those
without a voice
to make that choice
self-censure
and the coward's ploy
retreat from noise.

June 24th
TEXT

little snickers
private jokes
not for sharing with those
you're seated next to
parallel reality
separate circles
you glance up from the screen
disturbed
to see me there
for real
a smile still ghosts your lips
from what you saw and heard just now
from someone in another room
another country, city, moon
the face to face with me
conducted at a different pace
one ear cocked
for signals
flashing lights
your fingers twitch
the eyelids flick
you have to write
to sign
to signal back
like semaphore through space

like Pavlov's dog
you leave this place
where you are seated
fly through the air
to where you'd like to be
because you can
you will, you must
respond immediately
in case you miss
the party bus

and later it is me
who finds you
through the air
when you are there
with someone else
with someone live
and I am disembodied
on your screen
and yet more real
than flesh and blood
than touch and feel
contained controlled
no need
for an immediate response
the ebb and flow
goodbye hello
of human conversation.

June 25th
PAIN AND RAIN

cockies in the trees
rain coming
steroids humming in the blood
to stem the flood of heat
that boils old bones
like chicken stock
bubbling on hot coals
grey skies leafless trees
the big freeze
my knees
are taking it in savage turn
to cramp my style
my crooked mile
the walking stick
stands laughing in the corner
at my vain attempts to creep
to side-step reconstruction
the saw the hammer
to crab to dull the stab
of pain at every step

cockies on the wire
wish that I could fly
higher than you do
to find the rain
to stem the pain
of flightless
fucked-up motion.

June 26th
TRAINING

winter fog football field
suburban training night
blurry guernseys under light
are fighting
blood-thick sisters for the ball
pony-tails jog steady
round the outer
coaches folding flaccid arms
cross yesterday's hard chests
and wish that No.6 would show some skill
while No.2's still ill
and No.14's torn a hammie in the race

winter fog and bitter chill
the circle tightens to a knot
no more drills
just focus focus focus
beneath the rising moon
the weekend game
is sooner than you think
the heat is on
but not inside the rooms
steam rising
from chafe-red hard-run skin
cold shower stings
endorphins kicking in
and everything makes sense
the game falls into place.

June 27th
ROW ROW ROW

morning mist
kayak carving creases
in the river
smooth brown long
the Maribyrnong
as chill as mocha slurpee
splish splash
oars dip
light as butterfly wings
right left, left right
insect-like
to cut a stripe
scissored through shot silk
moorhens coots
in two by two
mock your efforts
ibis gawk and crane
straining past you for
a glint of fish
cars on the bridge
a steady stream
oblivious to the flow below
flash of bike
a tram a man
in lycra

rocks as green as ogres teeth
close packed against the shore
no boats are moored
no sail-craft bobbing
Sydney-style
on some backyard marina
just you
in high-viz yellow
just a sliver
rippling river
in the shiver
of morning mist.

June 28th
CHRIST ON A BIKE

death hill rears up
and I see you
plummet down
to break your crown?
no just a bloodied knee
death hill
daily challenge
balance
will you ever get it right?
green bones
full flight
feel the thrill
of immortality
doleful parents sluggish in your wake
ache
for their salad days
of bike and skate
and picnics in the woods
scaling trees
the Silent 3
the clubhouse in the forest
far from home
on our own
out 'til dark
in the park
on the swings
on the slides

hanging by the knees
circusing trapeze
and made up dreams of shows
starring only
little me
by myself mostly
alone and unafraid
something you could never know
never get to play like that
never understand
as you plummet
uncontrolled
to the bottom of death hill
screaming
never knowing where the brakes are
never seeing that the power
is in your hand.

June 29th
LA MUSICA

"is this the pits?
dance you shits
is this the bottom of the barrel?
once more through O, Carol"
words I penned in desperation
one long ago Saturday night
into Sunday dawn
Manzil Room Kings Cross
in my green and fearless 20s
four sets to no one
and four sets to go
fast and slow
hot and cool
late-night punters yet to show
that was how we rolled
back in '78
pay to play
house rules
up late interstate and hungry for it
whatever the stakes
no faking it
riffing true to the dream
nothing less than original
let 'em eat disco!
choke on satin and glitter
we raged unconditional

boiler-suited and dour
hour after hour
in the sweatshop of rock
zippered frock
cowboy boots
hanging tough
waiting for someone to call my bluff
desperate
to make it
time wasn't right
boogie nights
won the fight
then the punks
sunk the slipper
and I threw in the towel
one long cane toad Brisbane night
hung up the heels
and the glass tambourine
slunk away for a moment
away from the lights.

**June 30th
JUNE 30TH**

halfway mark
the spark
is still alight
I write each day
though
lately a few cheats
two or three to catch up
at a sitting
too much knitting by the fire
not enough rhyme in time
to make the deadline
never more than three
honestly
this poetry thing
has got me by the wrist
I will persist
in this
folly.

July 1st
THE DUDES

dudes
in mouldy dandruffed duds
still got the right to dance
to stand in rows
and jig in sorta time
they're out
and raging
on a frosty Monday night
outta mind outta sight
the old body's not so tight
wives and lovers
left so long ago
the kids are grown
these dudes are stoned
they're stoked
not even looking sideways
at the skinny vintage blondes
dancing two by two
arms held high
tight jeans stiletto boots
vodka eyes fixed upon the singer
the dudes have had their fill of sex
with some body else
dude eyes're focused on the singer, too

that singer is
the dude of dudes
rocks all their favourite tunes
invites participation
what the world needs now
is one more piña colada
voices raised
in beer elation
outside the mean street's quiet
a lockdown situation
so, one more shot, boys,
one more hit
before the short walk home
the dudes are dancing
drinking
living
in joyful
excitation.

July 2nd
30,000K SERVICE

un-car'd
unshelled
coated up
gloved and scarfed and
in the air
the arctic unconditioned air
commuters stare
into their phones
and talk out loud like Bedlamites
as if they cannot bear
to be alone
or look around
the world at 8a.m.
I hear ya!
it is bleak out here in tram-land
I don't know how you do it
every day
studiously ignoring the P.A.
warning
braking may cause sudden stops
what kind of un-brave
OHS world is this?
where's my connie
strap-hanging from the rafters
causing inappropriate laughter
at Tram Stop 53?

my car
my carapace
my cushioned throne
and instrument panel
my fingertip control
over all the elements
cocoons me
from the hoi poloi
the public space
the great unwashed
the face to face
I am soft vulnerable
turtle turned
exposed
on car service day.

July 3rd
RUBBER DUCKY

I am reborn
baptised
in steaming tub anew
I was lost
but now am found
to brood again and stew
in pleasant waters
deep
at first I was afraid
I was petrified
I thought I'd lost the knack
of lowering my crack
to reach the surface
without flooding, slipping
scalding
lying naked in disgrace
thought I'd break
on the way in
then drown before
I figured the way out
but all is well
I am renewed
a big fat nude
with knees more knobbled than
last time I soaked
but they came through
post-stew
those bones
they took the weight
of steaming me
on all fragile fours
climbing out
they did not fail
or slip or flinch
and now I know
bathtime is not lost to me
(rhymes with colostomy)
one of life's necessities
is back within my reach.

July 4th
SPACE

empty mind
it's what the yogi strives for
it's how you find
the next idea
between the ears
inside the soul
tumbleweeds roll
across the frontal lobe
magpies caw
waves lap upon the shore
listen!
a pin drops on carpet
and no one is at home
all the lights are on
and I am in the zone
where no thoughts roam
free range
blank page.

July 5th
GRAYSON PERRY HOUSE

art is no mystery
art is family
the how the why the what
of mum and dad
the good and bad
of kitchen sink
of birthday cake and Christmas Eve
sisters brothers
cousins grandmas
living dying
going bananas
the house the flat
the semi-detached
the walls the windows
floors and doors
that made
you
stick figure in a landscape
echoing sounds that tuned your brain
to handle pain
and dream of pleasure
expectation
hope
and disappointment
love and loss
lust and disenchantment

it's all about the hearth
the slap the kiss
the Sunday drive
the picnic in the park
making sense of life
and life is family
family life
la sagrida família

I don't know about art
but I'd like to know
why
I like what I like.

July 6th
THE MUMMY

farewell
on a windswept plain
beneath a chilly sun
the hole yawns
fakely fringed in green
feet totter on the spongey grass
in cramped stiletto heels
bought fresh
to honour her
with style
your hand
cannot, will not
loose the rose
to let it fall
to tumble hollow
to the box

you held it
so together
made it nice
made it graceful, funky
just as mama would've liked
but now
the mud is real
the smell is on the breeze
and in your mouth

the sweet pale coffin
lowers to the pit
and you are wrenched
and wracked
your hand cannot
loose the rose
cannot say goodbye
forever

I know this play
but not this scene
my mother, too, was stolen
even younger
I did not get to see the hole
the flames
or say the words
or choose the tune
or roll the pictures
light the candles
grip the handles
walk her to the car
I did not get to say goodbye
like you

there is no good day
to cut the tie
to wipe the eye
and know one day
it will be
you.

July 7th
ON DRUMMOND ST

my tower room
long gone
fell to the wrecking ball
and crushed four men
beneath a wall
into the cut-price bargain
to make way for more shops
my window on the cop shop
late night thrills
a door torn off
a moving car
dogs in hot pursuit of crims
communal front door wide unlocked
home ajar to street scum
friend and foe alike
at all times of day and night
visitors guests
overstaying tacit welcomes
bags fuller when they left
than when they came
late night jests
around the manky table top
scent of baking pot
gaslight hot
the whoosh of flame
to wash the dishes
no MAN ever washed

my tower room
hard by the courthouse
I never had misfortune
to appear in any guise
on that bleak stage
before the beak
and could not seem to walk
the few short metres
to its door
to see a show
until tonight
and it is cold as justice here
bitter winter night
and not a wig in sight
the pews are gone
the judge's throne
carved wood, tomes to swear by
showbiz in a softer form
now struts its stuff
in this deconsecrated and
repurposed room where
courtroom drama
once was the only show in town
and it feels wrong somehow
and yet so right
these old walls ring out better
than some sterile hi-tech box
devoid of history or of class
a theatre built to last.

July 8th
BIRTH

dreaming of The Rock
I'm always swimming
running late
to catch the plane
explaining
where my cases are
and how I need to board a ship
right now!
on the side of the road
at the pointy end
ocean all around
and I want to take a swim
in the river
(there are no rivers here)
at the beach
stands to reason
makes sense
I took a long time coming
she said
big head
pulled out of the water
on the side of a rock
I am wallowing
in false memory
of Gibraltar.

July 9th
THE DRIFT

sleep
or is it stupor
Lethe or the Styx
Sandman or Chiron
who pays the ferryman
oblivion or rest
the undertow
has me in its drift
like twelve small boys and coach
escaping
from a cave
being brave
against the odds
against the current
in the belly of the goddess
her broken stony heart
I am in the river
of life.

July 10th
TOUCH AND GO

intimacy
it's a tricky thing
the public face
the private space
the hug, the air-kiss
no-go zone
the brush, the flinch
leave me alone
lovers leap
to inhabit one another's skin
soon fades away
like mist among the trees
it does not last forever
by small degrees
the pressure of embrace
shrinks to a shiver
until nothing's left
but memory
of kisses kisses kisses
and of naked legs fast locked
and intertwined

you lose the habit
of the human touch
until
startled by a sudden arm
around your shoulder
the brush of someone's hand
you stop and ask
how did it come to this?
a stranger's touch
devoid of history
complexity
naked on the masseur's bench
soft moans escaping
unkissed lips
pleasure pain
the skin's remembering
intimacy
it's a tricky thing.

July 11th
HANK'S BEDSPREAD

'There was an old woman
tossed up in a basket
nineteen times as high as the moon.
And where she was going I couldn't but ask it,
But in her hand she carried a broom.'

craft
a witch in flight
across the face
a crescent moon
immense night sky
spangled with yellow stars
and far below
a twilight twinkling
city silhouette

packets and packets and packets
of Patons 8ply
navy, cobalt and pearly grey
crochet
double-crochet turn turn
line after inky line
tedious as long-haul travel
my silver-edged planet
a separate disc
stitched in
witch adorned

busy hands never still
hooking in and out the months
until
I spread the vision wide
across my bed
(not yours, my son, for now)
in sheer delight.

'"Old woman, old woman, old wom-
an," quoth I
"O, wither, o, wither, o, wither so
high?"
"To sweep the cobwebs off the sky!"
"Shall I go with thee?"
"Aye, by and by." '

July 12th
BEDROOM BLESSING

sacred heart of Jesus
sweet heart of Mary
watch over my bed
from either side
of my Ikea heart
in lights
halos golden in the dark
of my disbelief
shrine to my longing
for order
and a plan
mother of pearl
beads told through fingers
with prayers
for this and that
in church I wore a hat
sometimes a cloak
a veil
the holy grail
almost had me
in its monstrance thrall

I miss all that
the stations of the cross
familiar tale of suffering
denial
and betrayal in a garden
with a brother's kiss

I do
miss all that
I miss confession
absolution
the lightness of the shriven soul
the sinless mouth
that kissed the wicked boy
last night
the tongue that darted in and out
now free and pure enough
to press the wafer to its roof
a clean sheet
and the weightless joy
of starting over.

Sacred heart of Jesus
Sweet heart of Mary
light heart of Ikea
watch over me
until morning appears.

July 13th
ROYAL BOTANIC

Australian eyes
are set to ant
what was that?
a bat?
a gnat?
splat!
get in first
before it hits
that speck might be a killer
bugs or tealeaves?
are they moving
do they quiver
cross the kitchen floor
shaft of sunlight?
maybe not
lines leading lacy
to a deadly knot
a furry eight-legged trap
snap!
alarm
constant alert

the gardens ain't a peaceful place
uh-oh!
what's this at 2 o'clock?
a nuff-nuff in a Carlton beanie
crabbing sideways
acting strangely
circling the lake
he goes

round and round and
up and back
possibly a loony
what's he up to?
why's he putting down that bag?
I sense a purpose
to that lazy jag
picnic families on the slopes
don't clock his Bob de Niro
Taxi Driver act
they're kissing, snapping
nibbling snacks
look out!
he's on the move again

this public space
for everyone
a jewel in Melbourne's spangled crown
is sewn so deep with memories
old and recent
fond indecent
work and play
drought and rain
the ducks, the eels, the lily pads
punting through the green and brown
the psychopath!
he's back and I am
outta here
my old eyes are set to 'fear'.

July 14th
BEDDY-BYES

bedtime
it's a workout
pillow here pillow there
beneath the knee
beneath the wrist
doona on doona off
up down up down
halfway strewn
in a ruck
you're hot
you're not
feet in socks
ice to fire
static crackles
spraying dry hand sparks
across the slinky fake fur throw
gotta go
to pee
again
at regular two hour sittings
to check the pulse
to check the time
heart racing and
red numbers blinking

we once lay naked
locked and fucking
hot and panting
until we drifted off
like logs
floating down cool rivers
to wake
to kiss
renewed and rested
welcoming morning light

back to rearrange the pillows
cushion aching joints and bones
right and left
but nothing's right
right up to the bathroom light
next door
flaring up at 6 a.m.
the pillow dance begins again
does the pain
require drugs?
scrabble for the Nurofen
the Panadeine, the Panadol
suck the trusty water bottle
7a.m. sleep comes at last
to wake at 9
exhausted by the struggle.

July 15th
FINLEY

the dog
clipped on my desk
in a photo
permanent reminder
I didn't love him enough
sweet dog
sop to my children's need
for pet
thought I could rationalise you
contain you
exile you
and your ever-whirling fur
outside
reminder dog
of my hard heart
only seeing big brown shit
and the constant need
for food
sweet soul dog
perpetual smile
gimme a second chance
dog
to love you.

**July 16th
ROSIE**

the cat
wild child with a weepy eye
runt of the litter
in the saxophone shop
trailer-trash kitty
and witchy from the get-go
if she could've smoked
she would've smoked KENT
scrawny black grey
talons of steel
and an attitude the S.A.S. could use
lack of feely touchy
dead eyes at ground zero
weaponise
take no prisoners
ask for nothing but a dish of sprat
that cat
was snuggle averse
cuddlesome as a rattlesnake
survivor in captivity
6 months in an unknown location
reappeared meaner
leaner
PTSD cat
run over twice
attacked by rabid dogs and bats
ROSIE
no pussy
R.I.P.

July 17th
THE LAST TRUMP

a toddler
at the head of state
our fate
subject to baby needs
seems fitting
in this world
of toddlers, twats and temper tantrums
twiddling idle thumbs
playing games
naming names
engaged in self-styled settings
expansive as their tiny minds
can download to dream
confined by what technology
allows
they have no time
to contemplate a tree
they must upload
to make it real

the toddler
is the leader
we deserve
the selfie
we deny
the Masterchef Survivor
golden Idol
we all secretly admire

the age of thinking
good and bad
is gone
it is a ka-ka pee-pee
I want gimme-gimme
world now
where the toddler
the moron and the savage
ravage all
and straddle thrones
a simpler world
curated
for marshmallow minds
who want their data
and they want it now, Daddy!

July 18th
DOGGEREL

sky on fire
birds on the wire
a funeral pyre
Apollo's lyre
four flat tyres
I aspire
to make a liar
of your prior
convictions
I will not tire
will not expire
though there be dire
restrictions
cathedral spire
wheels in a mire
this pen's for hire
the widening gyre
a smoking briar
the wrong attire
mediaeval friar
climate change denier
will make a liar
of all
of your
predictions.

July 19th
ON YOUR KNEES

gymnasium
my happy place
where tired old bones repair
to mend
to spend time
in dolls' hospital
recovery suite
sweat is fat crying
muscles realign
reassert control
over chair
fear of stair
desire to kneel
to feel alive
and conquer pain
the hammer and the saw
kept at bay
another day
while we still can
stand.

July 20th
ARTICLES OF FAITH

read the paper
every day
news summarised
    verified
    authenticated
    minus the shrill
multiple
mini voices
clamouring
like puppies in a pound
digital now
old growth forests safe
a replica
of those pages
we once held
until our fingers smudged
is true to form
my town
not what the emerald city
decreed
that we lesser beings
should read
should know
stories in order
of weight

watch the news
on the box
unvarnished
slightly tarnished
by self-serving fluff
the right stuff
leaks right through

there are many ways
to skin a cat
I choose to be selective
about that.

July 21st
TWIT-AVERSE

expressing yourself
24 hours a day
I barely manage 2
and think
about what I'm going to say
and know
that I don't have to
stating
reacting
condemning
praising
damning
being clever
all day!
without pay!

I drop by the bird
from time to time
and all the beaks are
                absolutely
                totally
                continually
                doggedly
                perpetually
on line

get exhausted
clocking them
even for a minute
glad I don't need
to be in it
that my life does not depend
on what is trending
it's never-ending
a huge commitment
to the common voice
the common outrage
they're all so outraged
and so sad
tear)....
he/she was The Best
enough of that
back to outrage
and the gilt-edged
self-importance
of their thoughts.

July 22nd
FAMILY

life rolls on
straight as a wheelie bin
until you hit a random piece of dirt
and open up a seam
of long-forgotten weeds
that spring up from the cut
to coil around your ankles
nettle you with poison
spreading irritation
inflammation
rank infection
binding tightly both your legs
until you're off your balance
down
and sprawling in the mud
swimming in a rotting slew
of history
choking
on the half-remembered
buried hurt and lies
of family
kith and kin
you are sucked in
to the vortex
swirling just below the surface
of normality

civility
old battles
ancient scars
tears and deception
the past is in your mouth
and in your ears
like mould
like sweet primordial slime
time does not heal
it just gets worse
we should grow wise
as we grow old.

**July 23rd
SLOUGH**

torpor, torpor everywhere
nor any urge to think
to sink into the mire
embrace the cushioned chair
accept the drag
snuff the fire
lie down give in
despair
morning doubts
crowd in to banish
midnight good intentions
for action
and attack
and here you are
pyjama'd
after midday
on your back
wallowing in slack.

July 24th
CHINA BLUE

willow pattern plate
crumbs of what I ate
strewn like debris
in branches of your puff-ball trees
leaves
like eyeballs
in the doomed eternal garden
of lost love
o, turtle doves
the hand of fate
lies heavy on the barge
the bridge
the grim pagoda
gated park
encircled by a maze
the willow tree
and figures three
packing mystic weaponry
from which the lovers flee
beneath a smear of sauce
I spilled upon the crockery
as if in mockery
of what went down
in China
centuries long past
sad saga passed down
on a china plate
reminder stark in blue and white
resist unsanctioned
appetites!
or spend eternity
in flight.

July 25th
NATURE ABHORS A VACUUM

a journal of infinite possibility
stares up from my desk
to challenge me
with blank seductive pages
craving pen and ink
to scrawl out what I think
upon the empty space inside
where thoughts collide
invites me
to participate
like colouring in by numbers
write by letters
you can do it
they even have pictures
and quotes and clues
to get you in the mood
and maybe I will
one day soon
when I have run out of
everything else
I wanted to say
or do.

July 26th
SALLY DAWN

good friend
it doesn't end with a tiff
we are stronger than that
we are there
we are square
we are history
we go back
and we go forward
stumbling
joking
hurting, mending
sharing all the old familiar lines
on cue
campaigners in the culture wars
we are bonded at the hip
cursed by the lip
we often split
with bile and competition
but we last
to fight another war
and laugh to sobs
the shorthand of old gags
old bags
we are
familiar
thicker than family
on a good day
old friend
until the end.

July 27th
IT MUST'VE BEEN…

I see the moon
the moon sees me
not really
but I know it's there
over my shoulder
solemn white-face stare
with just a hint of smile
or is that menace?
grin or grimace
you decide
there'll be mayhem
on the streets tonight
a blood tide
in the half-light
of eclipses
mars and moon
will dip their headlights
while we sail on through their arc
like some upstart
ping-pong ball off course
dark thoughts will surface
just before bright dawn
steals in on chariots of fire
to clear the air
of what must transpire
tonight
in all that pink
and giddy
light.

July 28th
HEN

I still expect to clock
the ruby scooter
stationed at the door and
feel the fear
of your glint gimlet eye
och aye, hen
here she is again
in that old hat
to quell the crowd
who very dare
to speak out loud
while there's a ballad on

I miss you
in some indescribable way
like a phantom limb
the old street's not the same
it's not the same old scene
as when you reigned supreme
jazz mafia queen
with that
hard soft hard hand
upon the band
and kept us all in line
                                      in time
                                      in tune

slaves to a higher standard
none of us really knew
except through you
old bird
until we heard you croon
and bring us all to tears
and cheers
for one more chorus
one more
shit-pot, you.

July 29th
LAZY STOP-IN

the music plays
but I'm not there
to hear it
I am at home
I crave it
but I fear excursion
to that place of joy
no longer mine
to dig
in anonymity
scrutiny of a different kind
fraught with expectation
denial
judgement
fierce enough to flip my wig
will she, won't she
will he say 'hello'
that look of tension
tortured apprehension
of some kind of
scene
better I don't venture forth
to see my favourites
mill and floss
to gaze on me with
undisguised pity
'she used to be
didn't she?'

July 30th
JOLLY ROGER

my childhood hand
sketched pirate maps
skull caves
lapped by mermaid seas
dotted lines
to buried treasure
chest-deep secrets
where X marked the spot
and beware black spot
and rubied wealth lies in wait
to curse the stranger's slightest touch
doomed worlds
smeared on crumpled charts
torn edges charred
by Daddy's lighter
and stained with orange pekoe tea
those buccaneers
they beckoned me
with flouncy shirts
and cutlasses
and wild red beards
and golden earrings
to sail away into
their hidden harbour
where all is safe
and loyal and true
for that lawless, daring
handsome crew.

July 31st
JULY

so much for dry July
didn't even try
past those first five
sober nights
I blame it on the graveside scene
that gripped me
by the heart
in the most unexpected way
saw me rushing for the bottle
and the glass
and the glass
and the glass
and the tears
once they start
require continual drowning
downing
red after red after red
staggering to bed
to rise
to feel
remorse
aching head
self-disgust
until sunset rolls around
and suddenly
it's August.

August 1st
PINKO

friendship
it's the strangest thing
it cuts it binds
it is the strongest string
that twangs upon the heart
that sometimes breaks
when it is denied
or shunned
or somehow shoved
into the dark
and yet it thrives
to glow to shine
another day
and when it does
its strength is reassuring
comfortable
softer than the kiss of death
we are still here
together
and unlike the rest
we are peculiar
to a place and time
that is
forever
yours and mine.

August 2nd
UN AMI PERDU

you have slipped out of my life
like water through my fingers
in the slow lane
we traded stories
you and I
on those long trips
up the drama freeway
you were tender
thoughtful
smart and funny
supportive
somehow erudite
in hindsight
maybe
just polite
free ride
make nice
with other cats
you rocked a wilder style
and yet
I thought I
had your measure
knew what lay behind
your smile
seems I was deluded
excluded while
others colluded
to somehow paint me false
because
something happened
something I could not
explain
betrayal
treason
social gaol
exiled from your company
to cower in shadows
like some dirty dog
who'd chewed the master's shoes
then pooh'd
in full view

last time we met
by chance
you were polite
again
but this time with a cooler tone
a neon sign
leave me alone
old woman
we are strangers who
once shared a car
a stage
a laugh
a meal
no big deal.

August 3rd
THE MINX

beware the minx
she winks
but not in friendship
she is containing you
manipulating
think like the sphynx
ancient inscrutable
worn down but
commanding
historic
significant
magnificent to view
there are no links
between her and you
she will jinx the play
all the way
to misery and back
in fifty manic winks
don't kid yourself
you and her are not in sync
and you will come to grief
to know it
like you knew it
back in school
be not fooled
fool
beware the minx
and her toothy huggy
shiny bag of tricks.

August 4th (the fork)
THE GAME

up high
above green fields
I wonder why
I love it so
rain or shine
I have to go
to watch
to cheer
to scream
to jeer
the tiny figures far below
my big fat TV
slung above the winter fire
my creature comforts
call to me like Circe
my leather seat
no wind
no foul-mouthed crowds
no claustrophobic train
no foot slog in the rain
no mountain climb
zig-zagging concrete upward ramps
until you think you'll cark
from lack of oxygen
no knee dance down the row
no smart-arse loudmouths
who know EVERYTHING
and NOTHING

I could be at home
enjoying crystal vision
and no toilet queue
without my tribe
my yelling crew
of 'ball' and 'boo'
the roar of camaraderie
censure outrage ecstasy

that is why
I love it so
on crumbling aching knees
that is why
I have to go.

August 5th
PENTAMETER

reading verse
by famous poets
much much betterer than me
I find myself
confused mostly
except for the occasional stanza
that's a winner
that's so special
you begin to comprehend
the rest
why they're the best
and you are only scratching ink
at this late point
at this late hour
with so much to learn
maybe never learn
and yet
put pen to page
to scrawl
to rhyme
to speak in time
before it's time
to draw the line
to stop.

August 6th
IT'S NOT FOR ME

there be
dragons
beaks and feathers
hell bent for leather
wings protruding
leave me
cold as pudding in a bowl
what should be enthralling
is so dull
o, look! a troll
a robot on patrol
so easy to resolve
a sticky situation
with a door
a catch
escape hatch in the floor
you missed before
above the hidden river
in the cave below
flowing to the spaceship
transport to another zone
where it all begins again
ho-hum
is there no end to this
eternal
futuristic
unrealistic
doldrumistic
status quo

August 7th
WET WET WET

the sound of rain
steady pit-a-pat
street-wash spat drizzle
my chest drops
spine relaxes
synapses fizzle
and all is right on earth
beneath god's watering can
rare sightings will diminish
fade to memory soon
of times when all the world
was in whack
it won't come back
we pissed it willy-nilly
down the drain
we saw to that
with our insatiable desire
for hairspray
and a Frigidaire
and briquettes by the sack
police car sloshes through
the downpour
of some Nordic noir
and I could watch
that one shot
on repeat
flood-spattered street
of water
streaking down
soaking every raincoat wet
my body yearns for it yet.

August 8th
COLD

the swimming pool
opens and closes
summer thaws
what was frozen
leaves fall
black lace spines
pierce stone grey skies
and I feel fine
and cosy
in my coat.

August 9th
AVOWAL

the happiness gauge
cranks up to 3
I love you and
you love me
and nothing else matters
for now
we make the proper vows
to love
to care
to share
to be aware
of everything
that's felt
until we have to spell it out
in tears
after years
of happiness and
before
the drought.

August 10th
NESTING

let's build a house
a home
a place for us
to roost
to never be alone
a place where
everything is known
and shared
the stove
the bed
the bath
the credit rating
foundations made of stone
a no-fly zone
of total satisfaction
blissful interaction
from which
we'll never stray
except
to be alone.

August 11th
THE MONEYBOX

metal bird beak
tweaks the pfennig
elastic snaps
handle squeaks
and the money is ungripped
tipped slyly
into the raven crypt
where lies the treasure
hidden from my sight
the trick
of banking
in a clever toy
money pocketed by a crow
delivers
fun and joy
we are mesmerised by show
and never shyly ask
where did my money go?
load another pfennig
turn the handle
if you want to know
clever bird
to take those riches so.

August 12th
GYPSY JIVE

o, to be in Ireland
now that
anytime
is here
to roam the streets
in search of cheer
the half, the one
pretending I belong
strong ties
to none
to something hard
to put a name to
the constant need
for change
is in my bones
my DNA
a mobile home
room service
and a lick of strange
sea crossings
road trips airstrips
train travel
and another look at snow
I want to go
in search of shadows
ghosts and shades
once more to Dublin
Cork
and Galway Bay.

August 13th
PLUS ÇA SMALL CHANGE

life on hold
the penny drops
and I am in the red
once more
pretend poor
expensive roof above my head
food in the fridge
blankets on the bed
clothes in the drawer
safe in stasis
for now
rock the low profile
the cash cow
has wandered off
to find a greener field
the bluebird of happiness
is suddenly off-key
and won't be tweeting much
right now.

August 14th
SITTING

dress up for the camera
dress down for the paint
the lens never lies
the brush shows restraint
art is impression
don't matter what you dress in
what you decide to wear
which side to part your hair
the artist's eye
will see a different you

the camera is a bloodhound
sicked to sniff you out
expose
each hole
along your snout
each furrow blemish pouch
to construct a story
that is both false
and true
of you

the brush, the charcoal
paint and easel
will decide
which way to see you
see right through you
like the mirror
never does
oils will free you
separate the body
from the soul
parts become whole
an image
you won't recognise
as you.

August 15th
SAY IT NOW

don't wait until the deathbed
to say
I love you
or
I like the way you did so and so
it counts for more
to say it
in life
in day to day business
fork and knife
trouble and strife
never husband
not wife
don't wait to share
that fond moment
when you laughed to sobs
when you really cared
when all the petty bitchin'
day-to-days
got in the way
of shared

don't be scared
to open up to joy
man don't be a boy
life's too short
for coy
or holding back
embrace
the knack of living
every day
as if it were
the last.

August 16th
UNION ROAD

the milk bar
at the 10minute park
is gone
another little biz
moves on
and in its place
a frockshop
like we need another one
of those
like we need to buy
new clothes
more than we need
a pint of milk
the newsagent shut down, too
no-one reads the papers
anymore
they don't need a store
to keep up with the latest
who shot who
and what to do
and where's the war
the old shopping strip
is changing
like some Joni Mitchell hit
the council's rearranging
paving over it
carving out new streetscapes
for us elderly
they say

axing shady trees
to make walkways
'user friendly'
not in summer
they won't be
you need a tree
to cower beneath
in climate-changed
El Niño heat
in barren bleached
suburban desert landscapes
you need a place to sit
to rest your feet
and cool outside the Real Estate
sentimental fools like me
will need to buy a coffee
from some lactose-free
and pricey eatery
springing up in place of trees
in order to escape the sun
bask in air-con
for a neat four dollars fifty
move on quickly
back onto the blistered street

the wide old street
that used to be so
gloriously daggy
the milk bar
and its scarlet painted roses
on the window
are all gone
consigned to history
and the recent long ago.

August 17th
DOMESTICITY BLUES

dinner in the oven
fire in the grate
I come home late
as if I had a job
that paid
a bill or two
chicken or stew
who knew
my housemate could be
so accommodating
waiting
as the clock clicks round to news
he plays the blues
on instruments
designed to drive me mad
(he's not that bad)

the wine is red
how was your day
mine was okay
I tidied up
a paragraph or two
how about you
mine was fine,
too.

August 18th
MY SON

the need
to curl up
and moan
in
animal groans
grieving
the lack of you
and
the thought that you,
too,
might be hurting
and
I'm not there
to hold you
like nobody else in this world can
do
I am calling you
across the universe
to where you are
a suburb or two
away
lost to me
lost to you
come home
let me hold you
close
to me
do.

August 19th
SOW AND SOW

the sunflower seeds
are buried deep
within their bed of dirt
sun and rain
will do the work
to bake them
to perfection
green leaves peaking through
in time for sunny spring
a summer splash
of yellow
sent to cheer
the ending
of another year
rain and hail
presided at your sowing,
seeds
to meet your growing
needs
and speed your generation
from tiny tip
to universal
joy
and approbation.

August 20th
EDITING

grinding through words
in search of story
to find the whole
among the parts
the fits and starts
a through line
to the heart
of what you planned
to tell
the winding path
a passage
to the scene
the character you drew
you thought you knew
the way
the whole thing
would pan out
now doubt
and trepidation
requiring work
and dedication
to the task
until at last
you reach
The End.

August 21st
MERMAID

little girl in a pool
in a clear blue sea
half fish
half teacher
half made by me
little goddess
in swimmers
little mermaid
no flippers
we swam together
you and me
you in me
before you surfaced
to the world
before you came to be
water baby
always were
always will be
little girl in the ocean
in a pond
far beyond
in Croatia.

August 22nd
DENTAL CARE

the mask the gas
the smell of rubber
up dark stairs
the gloomy room
the headlight glare
electric chair
gushing water
instruments of torture
sharp on a mirror
my black and cola teeth
need work
must be wrenched out
by the root
from eleven year-old gums
I must lie inert
beneath the glass light
while evil fang-man
plies his bloody trade
pliers at the ready
needle long and hard
souvlaki skewer
poised and dripping
over my reluctant lips
to plunge to spear me
mother, spare me
don't sit quiet in your corner
mag and fag in hand
oblivious to my cries for help

not this time
I am up and running
bolting for the door
needle hanging from my maw
blood dripping on the fang-man's floor
I am gone
and I am running
running running running
down the street
to find the park
to crouch behind some thick trunked trees
waiting for the dark
slinking later
to the kitchen
cold and hungry
family shame
black teeth aching
breaking screaming
bite down hard
against the pain.

August 23rd
SPRINGTIME

take stock
uproot
weed and prune
the bud curls sweet
along the vine
gentle sunshine
on old pots
of yesterday's ideas
rusty shears
and secateurs
(my mother called them secateers)
another year
is pushing through the garden
leaf litter lying sodden brown
beneath the seething
worm farm
tiles need scouring clean
in time for pizza nights
hot buzzy evenings
round the table
soft carousing
under disco lights.

August 24th
HEY(WARD) HO(PE)

in the bubble
between
hope and trouble
between
faith and fate
rope dangles
hand grips rock
foot finds gap
you've been on this wall before
stood outside the door
with letters in your hand
your heart
must stay the course
must force itself
to fight all expectations
on this ride
prepare for the sick inside
when they say
sorry
not for us
not right now
thanks for showing
it's a no
maybe next time
in the bubble
for a while
you are drifting
on a tide of not knowing
daring
not
to dream.

August 25th
MONA VALE

the laurel is a lovely tree
emperor's crown
bay leaf for the stew
practical and regal
just like you
queen of needle, stitch and seam
we shared some houses
neatly as two pins
fond of gin we were
and music
and we laughed and laughed
at Woody
when he wasn't such a jerk
our badge of order
worn with pride
apple-pied
side by side
against a tide of mess
you made me dresses
showed me how it could be done
without too much ado
I salute you,
Laurel,
H.B. to you.

August 26th
METER MADE

"a penny in the meter
and the power was back"
I read those words
could hear the very coin
drop hollow to the box
see it squared black up
upon the papered wall
remembered still
the moment's chill
between the OFF and ON
between the light and dark
and I was back in some hotel
some long-term dingy seaside lodge
where we were dressed for dinner
breakfast, too
and sat up straight to face the plate
of porridge
compôte of fruit
grapefruit half with glacé cherry
in the English gloom
un-TV'd boarding rooms
between trains
and troop ships off to distant climes

my father in be-suited mufti
mother to the nines
shared bathroom
down the numbered hall
hard by the landing stairs
another penny in the meter
hot water in the sisters' bath
by turns
towel turbans
talcum powdered
stand in line
pink gas flame heater
until lights out
winceyette pyjamas
new from Marks and Sparks
a Lyons Maid fruit tart
saveloys pork pie
English home life
by the meter
1950s
that's what made me.

**August 27th
SOUTHEND-ON-SEA**

a slap of tide
against the pebbles
grey cold brine
froths up brown
to splash
green slime
rotting pine
wood beneath the jetty
ebbs out all the way to Kent
and boats keel over
on their sides
like drunks
resting 'til the sea sneaks back
to lick them up to rights
and all is mud
and slick and flat
crab pools glint
winkles wink
whelks and mussels in the drink
marooned defenceless
Southend Pier
a fat grey line
across the estuary
its end obscured in mist
like some Essex Yggdrasil.

**August 28th
BAD DRUNK GOOD DRUNK**

man I heard
downs a bottle of vodka
a day
makes me feel suddenly
okay
about my habit and
anyway
I've never even sampled
vodka
makes me feel epicurean
in taste
selective in manner
piss elegant
in my comparatively moderate
practice

a bottle a day!
spirits him away
to a status higher than
this lowly wino
but then
what would I know?

August 29th
THE MASTER

piano down below
yawn at the door
the master is home
time to watch some more war
hard worker, he
deserves every break
and lie-down
he can muster
protestant work ethic
happily combined
with job satisfaction
makes for a life
content
he's got it sorted
two houses bought
and every penny safe
not complacent but
he's got it made
he had a plan
this tired happy
yawning
good hard-working man.

August 30th
THE NIGHTLIFE

shops by night
windows bright
shadows and light
you never sight by day
when all is drab and flat
and dusty globes
thick smears of fat
are banished after dark
when all the lamps are lit
showtime!
action!
costumes wigs
and scarlet lips
flashing eyes
swaying hips
technicolor diorama
drama
the switch is thrown
to life
and everything makes sense
along the strip
wild streets
you roamed 'til dawn
light-footed
in your platform heels
and satin shorts
and stockings torn.

**August 31st
LYGON ST**

buzzy buzzy
night wet street
purpose purpose
people meet
in search of pleasure
search of love
drive drive
strolling parking
marking time
outside the club
inside the bistro
trees above
shake off rain
seen it all before
heard the laughter
the bus stop
and the ugly brawl
ice cream parlour queue
who knew
banana split
would be so hip
with this eclectic crew
twenty thirty
all allowed
to lick as much ice
as they like now

beanie babies
what to see
what to do
this way that way
right at you
high-heeled ladies
low-heeeled spivs
moustached and waxed
bearded, too
it's all go
no stop
hip hop
chop chop
gliding streaming
tell and show
on this wet gleaming
late night road.

september....

September 1st
IT MIGHT AS WELL BE

first day of spring
ring-a-ding-ding
it's raining
I'm not complaining
that's how it oughta be
wet dry hot chill
works for me
springtime baby, me
Spanish spring
deep blue sea
below the Rock
the pig the boat
my Daddy's knee
perpetual spring
would work just fine
temperature no more than 23
sometimes less
loose cotton dress
balmy nights
chill negroni
gin and lime
never enough to raise a sweat
warm dry cool
occasionally wet.

September 2nd
FATHER

fathers' day
the old one and the new
the dead one and the now
vying for attention
in our hearts
and in our souls
rough feelings
bubble up
to break the surface
of the glad-wrap
we have stretched across
the wall
of pain
the lost child
the serpent at the breast
who fangs
and fangs and fangs
with unrelenting blows
until the poison cuts
erupts
smashes through in waves
and we are drowned once more
in his ice cold
disdain

on this day
when we remember
our soft fathers
gone before
I long for some small quiet chat
a natter
a cup of good strong tea
with that reclusive man
and then
I look at you
and see
a good man here
a good father
loyal and true.

September 3rd
CLOG

are you still alive, Clog?
rock-dogs drop like flies
the sixties take their toll
for the 60s
sex and drugs and rock 'n roll
roosting
like so many chickens
flying home
does anger still sustain you, Clog?
is rage
still fending off
the reaper
for another year
it must be such a bummer
to find yourself
alive
and kicking
after all that beer
you who were so lean
so taut
so tense
muscle-trained and ready
for attack

the silent assassin
knife in the back
traitor's betrayal
and for what?
exactly
to live is to suffer
'l'enfer, c'est les autres'
I think of you
from time to time, Clog,
but not enough to call
my head has had enough brick wall
why risk the lash
the guilt
the tears
the scorn
but now and then I wonder
are you still alive, Clog?

September 4th
SUEZ CANAL 1960

deckrail
looking seaward
liners in the harbour
queued and ready
look! the Queen Mary
assembling quietly
orderly patiently
in the Bitter Lakes
to make the narrow trip
strip torn
straight through
tight sand passage
dry wet dry
unfriendly
unseen eyes
ancient lands of pharoahs
and of war
sliding silent
carefully
between white grainy shores
smooth glide
wet dry wet
not a soul for miles
business as usual in Suez
fragile negotiated trust
sitting ducks
human cargo in the dust
that was us.

September 5th
ASTRAL WEEKS

I used to track the stars
for love
heavens above
will he won't he
does he don't he
three coins, too
for love
will he won't he
don't he do
love's questions
answered now
the bear the plough
I track the stars
for gold
news of money
better times
employment
bank roll
change of fortune
cash cavalry
fiscal relief
wealth beyond belief
I have no need for love
or dreams of Romeo
and no longer throw the coins
I spent them
long ago.

September 6th
H.B J.K.

tears well up
I see you
in the jacaranda sea
of blossom
in the bloom of health
too soon to fade
to sink beneath the wave
of life
despite the stars
despite the will
to fight the grave
still beautiful
crooked smile
upon those lips
that once poured forth
sweet melody
with me
laughed that sharp
staccato laugh
as if surprised
and sometimes gave me curry
odd couple
you and me
same different
trash zen
Jane and Jenny Wren.

September 7th
NO WARNING

bad child day
tears come
they won't go
because you know
you've lost the child
forever and
all it takes
is a flash
another child
not yours
but like
to remind you
of the loss
and you ache
for just a glimpse
a little sight
of the kid
just a minute
maybe two
for a view
just a minute
and you'd promise
not to
reach out
not to
speak
brush a cheek

bad child day
the kid is lost
away he ran
and
if you see him
one day
he'll be grown
be old
be nothing
short of
a man.

September 8th
JASMINE

jasmine in the air
a thousand doors
swing wide
Fitzroy springtime
cotton frocks
bike rides
and dreams of love
happy hippie houses
full of life
full of conflict
conversation
melody
and freedom
deep in the night
waiting for the car
the gentle rap
upon my heart
and kisses that don't stop

jasmine
neverlasting
but so strong
my mother on her Sydney deathbed
in September
by October
gone.

September 9th
GLACÉ

ice cream cliff
of lovely palest green
scraped up hard
against a pillowed rose
beige-ly scrunched and berried
scoop spoon buried
to the hilt
Excalibur stuck fast
out-slid at last victorious
to dig
to lick
to poke about
in cone or cup
it matters nowt
crisp or waffle
chocolate truffle melt
drips down dribbling
to the elbow
sticky digits
sucked with
honeycomb and passionfruit
tongue sculpting
order
on the alps
of dairymaid indulgence
brain freezes over
in the rush
to slurp
sweet paradise.

**September 10th
SOFTLY SOFTLY**

the door is wide
outside blows in
and winter takes a bow
goodbye for now
did'ja like me?
well, so long, mate
time to hibernate
no more fire
in the grate
ashes swept
and firewood safe
until next May
Jack Frost, be on your way
Royal Show posters on display
to pipe the season in
Barnsey, jam and showbags
every cow will have her day
every brat their roller coaster
racing neddies neigh
the cricket's on its way
warm breezes
sneak through the shutters
time to clean the gutters
summer's coming
help me, Jesus.

**September 11th
PATSY**

pearly face
two-burnt-holes-in-a-blanket eyes
you made my year
with your reply
to my extended hand
of cosmic sisterhood
of service-brat-is-hood
we spliced a bond
we saw the same
and made sweet friends
if only for a mo
that's all I really wanted
all I asked for
and you gave it,
Jo.

September 12th
REFLECTION

mirror mirror
who is that?
is that me
am I that fat?
am I that spotty
droopy bald
am I still here?
(cue mild applause)
then suddenly
o, joy, o, glee
there's recognition
I see me
I know that face
I smile at me
I'm so relieved
to see me there
the girl I know
amid the glare
and I don't care
how old the face
how thin the hair
as long as I can spot
a trace
of how and what
I used to be
I am content
with what I see.

September 13th
GOD'S TEETH

god's teeth
were they/are they
all that sparkling white?
frightfully
symmetrical
row of tombstones
carved from Harpic'd toilet bowls
dazzling they are
celestial
unnatural
as god's teeth
might be
but does he/she/it
need teeth/
to eat
to gnash
to gnaw
to grind
to bite
to snap
to chew
to flash

at unsuspecting you
like pearls gouged
from deep oysters
like we mortals do?
I would say not, god
but those players
on my TV
need them brilliant 32
unstained
by wine
or food
or ciggies
as if they never lived
or dined
or slurped at tea for two
as if expensive dentistry
flagged immortality

'alas, poor Yorick'
thine choppers
are a-blinding me.

September 14th
THE WEIGHT

fat or thin
within the skin
what should matter
is your peace of mind
the only one to please
is you
no one gives a flying fuck
about the work you do
to fit within the dress
happiness
cannot be measured
by the skinfold
by the kilo
thin is in
inverse proportion
to the need
for what?
internal standards
make the call
and you will not be happy
'til they're met
you just don't get it
no one cares about this shit
but you.

September 15th
FAMILY TIES

linked by DNA
inherited connection
with more holes
than scratchy pink tulle petticoats
enmeshed
and yet
as distant as the milky way
random
as a scientific test
genetic markers
manifest
and yet obscure the join
we are as
unrelated
as badgers are to gnats
we catch a glimpse
of something
slight familiar
but within a flash
it's gone
and we are on our own
once more
we are but one
singular
peculiar
and queer
as home-made beer.

September 16th
FLASH

a moment
a could've been
across a café bench
strangers eating
studiously
avoiding but aware
at such close quarters
then first word
then flood
of shared

a moment
he was lovely
I was old
but it was something
like my salad
it was
enough.

September 17th
FIRST CARS

my first car was a Holden Premier
maroon De-Luxe HD
scored for free
and gifted by HT
pop legend friend
he dumped it
round in Pigdon Street
left keys
and no instructions
fucked back off to Sydney
on a promise
of bigger better cars
managing some rising stars
I'd be doing her a favour
if I took the bastard
off her non-driving hands

my own car?
sweet jesus save me
I did not need that much persuading
the rego wasn't due for ages
plush seating
and an AM/FM
automatic
very grateful

my bikie days were ten years gone
I pushed a Raleigh
shared some bombs
but none would get me out
to work on time
to Channel 10
in far off Nunawading
that metal monster
changed my life
I drove it 'til it stopped
until the tow truck
winched it up
and took it to the tip
down to its dying kilometre
and oily extreme unction
and I had spied another legend
a '65 XP
a golden Falcon
gleamed at me
from the window
of a dealer
in St Kilda Junction.

September 18th
SLEEPY TIME

the body sleeps
to heal
it will not be denied
the head lies heavy
on the pillow
sand lies heavy
on the eyes
closed
for repairs
you are
out of order
schedules out the window fly
and you are sucked
into the vortex
of unconscious weight
you have to wait it out
and bless the notion
that you have a choice
the inner voice
commands obedience
to embrace this
stasis
while
repair cells move in
do their work
to stitch
to fill
to patch
to quell
to paper over cracks
while you are
stretched out flat
exhaling zees
upon your back
in restful, healing
slumber.

September 19th
ME AND I

there are 2 me's
who never meet
they are discrete
7p.m. me
and the one at 3
a.m., that is,
scared in the dark
and in a sweat is Mrs 3
with racing heart
and imminent death
a definite possibility
Mrs 7 cannot wait
to down a lovely wine
Mrs 3 swears tonight
was the very last time
Mrs 7's a guzzler
Mrs 3 teetotal
memos sent by Mrs 3
could not be more convincing
'You're killing yourself!
Think of your health!
You really must stop drinking!'
Mrs 7 does not check her Inbox
is shy of detox
does not count the glasses
she's drinking
it tastes so good
haven't drunk that much
no time for any
clear thinking

I wish Mrs 7
would listen to 3
come up with some arrangement
to keep 7 happy
not out of control
and free Mrs 3 from danger.

September 20th
SKY-SORES

prongs
of glass and stone
sky piercing
gagging for attention
men
bent on immortality
for no imagination
'let's make it green!'
'let's splash some purple!'
to mask a total lack of style
'our steeples will be seen
for miles
as genius'
by some people
others, not so much
completely out of touch
they are
with what makes the world
go around
go around
tall thin columns
thrusting up
from ground
like monumental dicks

The Concrete Age
of bland and boring
cranes and pouring
vibrant as a spread-sheet
riveting as banking.

September 21st
FINALLY

young men at their peak
smooth-cheeked
this day will not repeat
this prime of life
each muscle sleek
and oiled
caressed by experts
a dozen options for the hair
short long
beard bun
alice band and
retro razor chic
the tattooed sleeve
vaults through the air
aloft on faultless knees
crashing to the turf
with ease
without a care
the hopes and dreams
the boos the cheers
of more than ninety thousand fans
are ringing in your ears
the taunts the jeers
hearts pumping
ready for the fray

the skinny seconds tick away
like time bombs
flying feet and
god-like feats
of supernatural strength
bursts of speed
turnovers on a zac
rebounding from the pack
like coca-cola yo-yos
the siren
and the tears
the sporting handshakes
while the body reappears
and every knock and hit lines up
to say g'day to you
oo roo!
but you knew
immortality
for just an hour or two.

September 22nd
STALKIE

I have a pen-friend
in the States
I've never met him
in the flesh
but somehow
we are mates
Facebook Friends
(the truest kind)
and I don't think
I ever want to meet him
face to face
because he seems so nice
we laugh
at all each other's jokes
and tick
each other's Likes
each other's politics
we've traded books
and real CDs
but maybe
the living breathing
he
would be
too much
I do enjoy his comradeship
I think
that is enough.

September 23rd
RECIDIVIST

in the rapids
above Niagara
Mrs 7 strikes again
like some demented goldfish
floating
drifting
in the current
Joseph Cotton down the lens
sings
'Oops, I did it again'
in fateful resignation
to the coming storm
an eerie silence hangs
before the pounding falls
annihilating cataract
of deep stupidity
no turning back
the die is cast
you drained the glass
down to the last
and you will wake
most certainly
disguised as Mrs 3.

September 24th
WALKIES

house dogs
straining at the leash
dragging minders
down the street
like big fat meat on strings
they want to run
to bite
to bark
to pee
to sniff another doggy's bum
for clues
they want to go where doggies go
without you
and your string
your ball in that stupid plastic thing
to do their own wild canine thing
eat children
frighten cyclists
shit
out in the open air
anywhere and everywhere
they just don't care
about you
you should know
you who buys them sawdust food
instead of blood-soaked treats
that they can
chew and chew and chew
like they're designed to do
they have the teeth
the thick red tongue
you think they care for you
and your
soft fluffy toys?
who knows
maybe they do.

September 25th
LIFE 1

toilet rolls and Vegemite
such is life
squares of paper
squares of toast
on and on
unfurling
until it tapers down
to shit
get over it
and buy another pack
a jar
and don't look back
don't look as far
as your behind
I think you'll find it
far too real
yank on the reel
and face the facts
the grand design
of life
is tea and Vegemite toast
a glass of wine
a Sunday roast
a balance of the in and out
that is what
it's
all about.

September 26th
LIFE 2

sex and real estate
such is war
that way
Armageddon lies
no keeping dicky in his flies
or coveting your neighbour's pile
the history of the world
comprised
within these two
grim markers
civilize it all you like
these two will not
find respite
in peace
where's the sport in that?
save it
for the long and boring
afterlife
meanwhile
this old mortal coil
has needs
desires
that can't be tamed
can't be assuaged
stop pouring petrol on the flames
stop trading blame
the game of life's
the same old same.

September 27th
LIFE OF ME 3

ten years forward
seems so short
ten years back
like yesterday
time's running out
to get things done
to see my son
can't think in years
or else the fear
will do my head in
keep me up
at night
in fright
when I should be
sleeping.

September 28th
ME AND THREE

blood is thicker than water
four daughters
several fathers
a row
of paper cut-out dolls
strung far apart
straining
fragile
complicated links
swinging in the breeze
of life
we smell the same
don't look the same
or talk the same
we know the names
of things long dead
as we
in time
will be
me and those other three
selves
genetic serendipity
brought us to this place
we are as one
three are not me
and yet we
are as one
it cannot be
undone.

September 29th
HOSSIE

hospitals
don't frighten me
all monitors and beeps
and tilt-up beds
and laundered sheets
and nurses
noting every impulse
constant checks to see
if you're okay
you're still alive
they're never far away

and they will listen
to your fears
they are all ears
they take you seriously
bring you endless cups of tea
escort you off to have a wee
and tuck you in at night
beneath the eerie fluoro light
where life takes flight
and life alights
like angels
on the shuttlebus

with luck
we all will die in bed
surrounded by trained staff
and graphs
of heart-rate, pulse and
opioids
dripping through the stent
to ease us through
from hospital
to something
new.

September 30th
SO GRATEFUL

I am
a very lucky person
I live
in a nice house
I have
my health
despite scant wealth
I have
no lust
no need to please
or to impress
I just
get on with it
the daily biz
a cryptic quiz
or two
some tea
a calendar of shoes
and then a coffee
with my friends
some driving
writing
marrying
burying
then a wine at seven
I may
complain a lot
but, really,
this is heaven.

October 1st
LUSH LIFE

two bottles of red
a night!
I feel so righteous
I may have another glass!
look at me
with my less than one bottle
limit
I'm practically teetotal
by contrast
to my secret swilling
elder sister
two whole bottles
at one sitting!
and it's not even Christmas!
I'm in a coma
after even half a neck
and wracked with guilt
shiraz transgressions
pre-dawn confessions
and constant, shattered resolutions
meanwhile
she is guzzling for Australia!
bestowing alky absolution
upon my paltry efforts
to rise up to her spirit level
of certain
kidney failure.

October 2nd
ANNIVERSARY SONG

full moon over Sydney
36 years hence
a fumble on a motel bed
embarrassingly gauche
and here we are
together still
through ups and downs
through wine and gin
through fat and thin
through tears and grins
together
but
apart.

October 3rd
FLAGGING

friendship wine
Father Time
there must be more than this
to versify
remembered kisses
babies crying
through the night
for something
who knew what
not me
novice mother
almost forty
learning on the job
did what I could
only
to see it end in sobs

September bolted into Spring
and I am running out of juice
for inky scrawls across the page
to stay the course
enough
to prove some point
to say 'I did it'
everyday
to bray
I did not pike
to testify
I did not flunk.

October 4th
STUFF

roses roses on the fence
around the rubbish dump
of psycho-clutter
relocated
can you not separate
the treasure
from the trash
do you not see
the mould the dirt
the mash-up and the mix
of flotsam jetsam
no one in their right mind
wants to keep
they threw it out
upon the slag heap
of detritus
and no amount of talking up
of distant pseudo-royal connections
will rescue it
or value add
or save it
quite as much
as you would like it to.

October 5th
FLORA

cut flowers in a vase
we try
to capture them
for life
first plunge in water
and they're on the road
to ruin
to the bin
snip them
snap them on our phones
preserve them
fresh
for all the world to see
their beauty
their simplicity
in the midst of bloom
they are in doom.

October 6th
TO – THE LARGEST ORGAN

the skin
taut for milliseconds
in the scheme of things
pink and springy
firm and moist
until
unbidden
spots appear like flies
lines and rings around the eyes
deep shipping channels
in the cheeks
a testament to
laughter
and to life
that we should honour
praise and thank
instead of mewling for the knife
the needle bearing toxin

the moment goes
the window closed
on what we did not know
nor treasure
when we had it.

October 7th
THE MOUSE

there's just the one mouse
no?
we see it
and we know it straightaway
him/her/mum/dad/it
white with pink bits
right?
twitching nostrils
gagging for it
blindly eating
sniffing
touching
trying
everything
that comes its way
into the tank
from down the chute
so clean
so pure
so white
so cute
a trillion squillion mouse soldiers
treadmilling
in the battle against death
and yet –
there's just the one mouse
yes?

October 8th
MUMMY AGAIN

your face in the sky
I wonder
do they let you do that
for today
the day that marks
the day you went away
at least I now know
where you lie
scattered
in Rose Garden B2
who knew
not me
a little earthy bed
to come and visit
when in Sydney
who'da thunk
you'd end up there?
of all the places in the world
you lived and breathed
and had affairs
Kanpur to Botany
what a wonky trail
of empty bottles
gin 4711
filter tips
diamente clips
fake fur
rollers silks
lovers babies
lover's baby
and the ones
that didn't make
that cruellest cut of all

I see your face in cloud
and sense you all around me
through me
in me still
I am your girl
the one who loved you best
rest rest
I'll never love you
less.

October 9th
HERE COMES THE SUN

Summer's sneaking in
on bloated swollen feet
I see ya
feel ya
trying to smuggle in the heat
that will defeat me
teasing with fair temperate days
blue skies
soft breezes
to shoo the winter dark away
"boys and girls
come out to play
trust me
it'll be okay"
you say
"I won't bite
I will not burn"
but I know how
this scorching saga
tale of woe
will headlong go
to suffocation
thirst
and sleepless nights
and sweating sweating sweating
like chopped onions in a skillet
and we must gird our unclothed loins
to grit our teeth and bear it

o, blessed Spring
you lovely thing
perfect as a budding rose
I don't blame you
for the company you keep
your Autumn twin
scored a much cooler pal
I know your dark and lethal secret
the hidden flames
the burning soles
parched grass
and melting roads
stand waiting in the wings

we wind the clock
an hour fast
and brace ourselves
against
the fiery furnace blasts.

October 10th
NO BUSINESS

warm night
in spring
home quiet
remembering
8 shows a week
2 hours at a stretch
when I wore heels
had hair
and flawless skin
was thin, goddammit
when I thought I wasn't
climbed on tables
mic in hand
and, what's more,
climbed back down again
without a care
without pain
hard-working days and nights
affirmation
lights
applause
pleasure given
and received
bows taken
hands shaken

I earned my place
stood my ground
upon the lucky spot
of showbiz
and never knew
that some day
would find me on this couch
on this warm night
in spring
still able
but not called
yearn for it
as I might.

October 11th
STEP BACK A LITTLE

I like you
I do
but I'm going to step away
from you
too many 'ouchie' moments lately
when you fanged me
without warning
pulled the huff
some kind of rank
conflated stuff
that somehow made it look like
I was at fault
when clearly I was not
I don't want to
have to
watch my step
with you, friend,
you and your tight agenda
I'd be a fool
to think
I'd pass the test
give it a rest, mate,
I've been fucked over
by the best mate
and by the worst
and I'm too old
to bend
to shine your shoes

respectful distance
that's what's needed
now
I'm cutting loose
I'm striking cool
my stance
is one
of passive
resistance.

October 12th
NIGHT FLIGHTS

bright planes
black sky
bleeping in
from out
upon the hour
powering down
across my night window
blink blink blink blink
white red silver pink
reminders
of another life
another place
to go
to come
a stranger's face
to have been
to move toward
the world
and all its sights and sounds
winged transport
flapping

to and from
variety
and renewal
and escape
burn vapour trails
across my soul
harness
umbilical tether
to the need
for constant change
perpetual motion
to rearrange
this earthbound sludge
of repetition
parochial drudge
and
the same 'ol same.

October 13th
GONE

a Chinese bridge in Croatia
a rapper in the White House
another day
another battlement falls
and we stand naked
stripped of all
before the winds of dross
the death of class
the rule of cash
democracy of crass
we didn't get much Rome-time
before the Barbarians
were at the gate
with their Glocks and fries
the Doomsday Clock
ticks on
but we're already gone
for all money
in a baseball cap.

October 14th
COWARD

I was going to write
something
about racial stereotyping
something
about Rupert Bear
but then
I tied my pen in knots
trying not to write
something
that would offend
someone
somewhere
somehow
some way
it all seems
so clear
so straightforward
until the words
are out
into the light
of doubt
and you run away
in fright
of being
misconstrued
button your lip, girl,
no one really wants
to hear
any of that from you.

October 15th
WORLDWIDE RELIEF

there are places
like Poland
that are not
like us
old places
old buildings
old ways
local food that is
not
like ours
the world is not
the same
all over
no need
for despair
there are different
particular places
everywhere
away from here
we are not
the only
way to be
we are not
the only
reality.

October 16th
LOVE SINGER

listen!
she is singing of love
he is crooning of heartache
and
they don't know
what love is
have never known
what it takes
they are stone
they don't know
the meaning
don't have the right
to sing the blues
and we choose
to believe them
pay
to hang upon their schmooze
they are hitting the right notes
reproducing the tunes
they know nothing
of love
they are parroting
lyrics
penned by someone
who really did feel
those emotions
put pen to paper
put plectrum to steel

listen!
he and she
are musically
going through the emotions
of love but
when push comes to shove
they wouldn't know how to love
if it bit them
on the nose.

.

October 17th
MOURNING BECOMES

the wave of loss
it builds
and builds
until it breaks
up hard against
the stone cold wall
of ceremony
words are said
words we repressed
confined
held back
'til you were gone
and safely dead
and there could be no argument
no tears
recriminations
ancient grudges
put to bed

the wave of loss
breaks clean
across the deck
and you are washed
into the tide
into the wake
behind the ship
of life

we see you bobbing
for a while
think
we see you smile
we wave
then turn back to the task
of life
without you
and all that strife
of farewell
fades to
something new
something harder
than we knew.

October 18th
TOUCH

imagine
if someone
took your foot
in their hands
made it sacred
made it loved
revered
how would you feel
if your heel
could rest in a palm
with consent
be content
to be calmed
by the press of a hand
could be soothed
by the clasp of smooth
fingers
pressing your arch
stroking rough pads
and the dent in your heel
feel between
all of your toes
and not because you paid
for the thrill
how would you feel?

October 19th
AMARILLI, MIA BELLA

happy hippeastri
blooming in a pot
first none will come
and then a lot
it seems
arriving early to
surprise me with
bright trumps of joy
go forth and multiply
do
colonise my earthly beds
to shoot up clumps
of amaryllis on
sweet stalks of green
ballgown blossoms
billowed precision
a sultan's tent
on silken points
gold dust stamens
sugared wands
His Masters Voice
a garden dog
am I.

October 20th
NIGHT AIR

leather lying louche
soft steady breeze
wafts through the window
and across the couch
cool as salty waves on shore
I bask in air
inhale
the exhalation of the day
a subtle hint of rain
that's on the way
but for now
this temperate draft will do
the soothing honours
and require no throw
no cardigan
or cashmere wrapper
sudden change of clothes
it's so delicious
I could lie awake all night!
to feel this light caress
of ventilation drifting
through the flyscreen
refreshing as a waterfall
I surrender
warts an' all.

October 21st
IN THE PINK

pink gin
is in
my skin
to wash away the red
the scarlet and the dread
a lightweight fizz
it is
civilized and chic
avast the crimson curtain!
begone the shiraz gloom!
select a different glass
rose ranunculas in my vase
twenties flapper
I shall be
do the Charleston
cross those knees
sipping Gordons
cheery me.

October 22nd
SWEETIE PIE

just desserts
that's what you get
when I pull on the apron
engage the blender
heat the oven
Kitchen-Aid and spatula
and eggs eggs eggs
and sugar by the kilo
butter dripping
chocolate melting
double-boiling
stirring scraping
whisking in vanilla
shaking baking
soda
and cream
and cream
and double cream
until the custard
coats the spoon
berries scattered
cherries strewn
meringues harden into peaks

soufflés rise
the secret lies
in wanting
these sweet treats
for my mouth
why else would I
roll out pastry
knead the dough
gild the caramel
rocky road
to ruin
it's for you I squeal
and yet, I lie
I make it
just for me.

October 23rd
SHOE CALENDAR

the shoes are racing
page by page
in tippy heels and flats
the days will not walk back
the photos flap
the fashions flip
rubber soles and high
and boots
and zips
and ankle straps
gilded buckles
floral taps
and laces threaded
through blind eyes
my year is measured out
in shoes
of every hue
and style
in these broken
knock-kneed days
it makes me smile to
see each month
roll out the pumps
the mules, stilettos
and the trainers
while I hobble
in my clogs
my pins
not quite so straight now.

October 24th
BAR

everyday a new bar
rows of bottles sparkle
punters packed
behind the glass
as if they'd always been there
sat upon those stools
and high chairs
they are
everywhere
new bars
where they weren't before
where once there was a bank maybe
post office, cobbler
butcher, record store
meanwhile
the corner pub
has disappeared
obliterated
pulverised
by some guy
with real estate eye
some guy
not from round here
some guy
allowed to do
whatever his fucking money
says
he'd like to do

you wanna drink?
go find a bar
they're everywhere
you won't get far
before
you see one glinting
at you
where the local cop shop was
dentist doctor lawyer church
sold up
and moved on
left the perfect setting
for a bar
another bar
exactly
what we want.

October 25th
RING-A-ROSIE

the roses
have come out to play
in time for Cup Day thrills
heady perfume fills the air
for free
in God's own Dior store
Mr Christian could not match
the shades
the texture
curvature
design
j'adore
each perfect spiky silk creation
the elegance
the sassy style
classic in delineation
photogenic masterpieces
doomed to peak
for just a week
all summer long
enough to make a person
question
earth and world
complexity
eternity
perhaps
I could be wrong.

October 26th
VIVA VOCE

I have the nerve
to stand up there
and do it
bask in coloured light
bathe in lustrous sound
peer through fog
at faces
looking back
and every note is heard
by me
in microscopic detail
no one else detects
defects
I feel to my very core
float past
their ears and eyes
crash to the floor
the slightest slip
my grip upon the mic stand
tightens to a claw
viva voce
the ongoing test
I'm glad to sit
to stand
while stand
I can.

October 27th
THE CULL

they drop down dead
like flies
there has to be a reason
for this killing season
every week another
maybe two or three
the well of tears
is deep
unfathomable
hearts like stones
fall to the bottom
with a muted splash
there is no drought
a rout by Mr D
is gouging souls out
just in time for
Halloween maybe
perhaps
and mostly chaps it is
too early
and too soon mostly
the blood-soaked piper
calls the tune

last drinks
last bus
lights out
so long
ta ta
goodbye
mud in your eye
kiss
heave a sigh
the rest of us
must do without you
and your fond remembered ways
the song upon your lips
the way you used to play
too late now
to banish bitter feuds
old grudges
and ingratitudes
the time is nigh
the tide is high
before we feel it start to ebb
in these grim and
grief-soaked days
old hearts can only bear so much
the business end of life
it cuts up rough.

October 28th
WHO'S GOT THE BALL?

why hate the queen
surely
there are bigger fish to fry
to wish they'd up and die
how does she
affect your life
down here down under
on a daily basis
okay
she's rich but
so is Gina Rhinehart
do you hate her as much
I don't give a flying fuck
for either of them
frankly
but one's more fun to watch
one gives good show
the other
not so much
you feel oppressed
for real
true dinks
be serious
it's time you had a chat
to someone from Pyong Yang
or Myanmar or Syria
a woman from the Middle East
try that

oppressed
by ostrich feathers on a hat
an accent you don't care for
half as much as
Father Ted or
Larry David
Patsy Stone
Steptoe or
James Brown
oppressed distressed
by power that wouldn't
scare a cat
power that doesn't stop me
doing anything
at all
the monarchy will fall
it's okay, relax
we will go all the way
of the USA
and we will cry
hip hip hooray
free at last
free at last
and welcome the banal
and realize
the queen
did not really
affect your little life
at all.

October 29th
'JUST A SMIDGE MADGE'

you set the tone
for us
a touch of androgyne
two fingers touch the lips
before the witticism slips
and lands
and cracks your face
and tips your head
and crimps your eyes
surprised at what you did there
almost camp
so unlike the crush
angelic in your youth
a way with words
a joking with the truth
halo of curls
set girlish hearts a-flutter
to no good
all misunderstood
in age
you sealed up tight so
hard to read

lost the skill to write
in ways we might
make sense
of the play
with words
went chasing after notes
as if that were the way
made me so cross
at such a waste
made me bite in haste
with my sharp tongue
and now you're gone!
and I long
for one brief moment more
to tell you
just how great you are.

October 30th
THE WHO-DO*

people try to put us
down
just because we're still
around
we were hot but now we're cold
we didn't die
we just got old

we didn't all
f-f-fade away
please speak up
I can't hear what you're
s-s-saying
I'm trying hard to get your attention
by talking about my
generation
this is my generation
light on veneration
my generation
we totally get your
condemnation
my generation
'don't need no hateration, holleration'
my generation
bay-bay-eh......

---

*with apologies to The Who

October 31st
MY ROOM

my bedroom
was a salon then
my worldly goods
since leaving home
packed and stacked
from wall to mantle
dress rack
book stacks
vinyl
knick-knacks
fruit-box bedside table

sat cross-legged on my bed
to throw the coins
to read the stars
and hope for love
a job, a car
candles weren't a thing so much then
ceiling lamps swung light and low
in lanterns made of paper
sandalwood and joss sticks burned
in purple mirrored elephants
knicked from Handicrafts of Asia

and guests would come
and sit and talk
and smoke
and maybe talk some more
the lounge was not the place for this
if, indeed, you had one
not a place to touch or kiss
corduroy sofa
black and white set
Canberra TV rental

we chewed the fat
around the stove
argued at the kitchen table
made cups of tea
and Bialetti
deep dark grounds
the price you paid for sharing

my bedroom
was my palace then
where I reigned supreme
on my $8 mattress
got little sleep
dreamed peaceful dreams
and revelled in sweet solace

no one sights my boudoir now
my padded cell
with fairy lights and
silken cushions
Spanish shawls
the door is closed
on conversation
curtains drawn
the heart-shaped bedposts
an ironic
loveless
symbol of what's lost and gone.

november....

**November 1st
THE CUTS**

to carve the flesh
for comfort's sake
to slice the skin
to trim the dress
like so much meat
just to be neat
blood must be shed
self-mutilation
requires a clear distinction
between mind and body
the idea of it
strikes so true
so right
so safe
so logical
but knives and needles
pain and scars
might induce guilt
regrets and scruples
lethal melancholy
we've come this far
my breasts and me
I can't quite see
a straight path through
to surgery.

November 2nd
MY FALLEN IDOL

Bomber Thompson on a bike
riding through South Melbourne
face set
low tide
looks like you just learned
to ride
and borrowed that two-wheeler
where the hell you been, Mark
to get so lonely
look so lost
weaving and unsteady
like the cops are on your trail

you were a god, Mark,
a leader
player
joker
and a spunk
before the junk
the low-life crew
and all their emptiness
moved in
to wreck you
rob you of our trust
and how we loved you

Bomber Thompson on a bike
I nearly rolled the window down
nearly stopped, Mark,
just to have a word
to try to cheer you
in your shabby jumper.

November 3rd
HOLS

holiday highway
such a long way
to the sea
to the shore
to the forest
to the trees
to the free to do whatever
fair or foul weather
and cook in harsh conditions
we sang in the car
together
no restrictions
no competition
as one
so much fun
and the little ones'd be asleep
by the time we spied the lake
and crabbed down the slope
to the shack
in the dark
and quiet night
in the valley
with the wind in the leaves
you and me and the moon
our little family
so happy
we.

November 4th
SUNSET CLAUSE

I suppose
I must strike something
quite ridiculous
eager readiness
ageing demeanour
imagining
I have some
kind of worth
with my girth
must induce mirth
wry appraisal
unspoken question
why?
is she still at it
why?
does she imagine
they would come
would pay
to see her play
or say some words
utter thoughts

I must accept
curio status
bow
to irrelevance
with a grace that
I have never been
famous for.

November 5th
ROSIE

rosé rosé rosé
the wine for today
shiraz, go away
take your heavy vibe
and shove it
I do not need
the weight
the drop
the darkness
of your tone
when I'm alone
and in my claret cups
jumping ship
I am
free of your logjam
in my physiology
and hygiene
(that's a joke from 4th form)
no,
I do not need
the wine dark stain
upon my addled brain
I am in the pink!
rosé, the drink!

November 6th
THE OFFICE

3 funerals and no wedding
tears shedding
for one of the three
due respect to two
we said adieu
instead of au revoir
or ciao
or see ya
to the dead
they have gone
on ahead
of us
pointing out the road
we all will tread
is not so lonely
or so dread
still an' all
they're gone
there'll be no more
additions
to their Wikipedia
their IMDb's up to date
sorted
and complete
the show reel ran
the song got sang
tune in for more
next week.

November 7th
PEPTO DISMAL

cheese
and chips
and battered fish
and ice cream
churning
in the squish
of my digestive juices
in the sluices
it's a battle
of a very fundamental kind
me v gluttony
with no winner
and no outcome
but for gas
and shit
it's the last thing
that a body thinks of
while shovelling
and guzzling
all those salty treats
seductive sweets
Mrs. 3a.m. has her alarm clock set
for an appointment
with my flabby heart
meanwhile I fart
try not to fret
or sweat
the Falstaff.

November 8th
RELIGIOSO

god's gone
kitsch lives on
in icons
cards and rosary beads
Infant of Prague
long brocade dress
and heavy crown
I confess to Almighty God
I cannot get enough
of all that
religioso stuff
madonnas and the flaming heart
of Jeffrey Hunter
King of Kings but
wasn't he a jew?
I bet that he
looked nothing like you, Jeffrey
Woody Allen
Jerry Seinfeld
Paul Simon, maybe
Netanyahu
as for Mary - well
virgin Mrs Joseph
I can't get enough of
rosebud lips
and blue and white
and hidden hair
and hands spread wide
in 'hey, it's not my fault' mode
this was the current dress code
the pictures stick like glue
and I can't shake them
off my shelf
my sense of self
even without god
resides in you.

November 9th
TODDLER

when he was mine
I ruled the world
my joy
my little treasure
soft arms flung
about my neck
unbridled pleasure

when he was mine
I thought the time
would never come
the day would never dawn
when he'd be gone
and I would wander
empty broken
and folorn.

November 10th
SISTO

stabbed through the heart
for kindness
care and grace
what random demon
led your blade
to that soft heart
the city's torn apart
with grief
howling up the length
of Bourke Street
Spring Street is awash
with tears
for Sisto
and his Fellini smile
his charm
his suave cravat
the friendly chat
that made you feel so special
like the strudel
and the pasta
madman with your flaming truck
you have carved our heart
in two and
all for nothing
all for you.

November 11th
SLEEP SCHMEEP

any point
in going to bed?
to sleep
perchance to dream
fat chance
an all-night battle
in two-hour parts
awaits
nightmare fits and starts
while my kidneys
crank up
wake up
punch the clock
get busy making piss
that I must wake to pass
at 2 and 4 and 6
unless
I am already up
and lurching for the couch
to douse the heat
to quiet the fear
to hear the possums
on the roof
to watch the minutes
ticking by
to see the dawn
and feel sleep come
past 7
by and by.

November 12th
MOMENTS OF DOG

I have moments of dog
when nothing seems more splendid
than the idea of dog
little face
tilted up
one ear askew
cutie pup
little chin to tickle
sweet companion
just for you
loyal and true
following after
to beg
a moment of your company
a mate
to throw a ball to
taking interest
in the slightest thing you do
a little friend
to love

then I remember…..

that attention
that dogged fixation
those needy eyes
and hungry teeth
full on
dawn to dusk
like a toddler
one that never naps
always needs a walk
and when it craps
that smelly shit won't bag itself
hair on carpets
fur on shelves
ticks and licks
and trips to vets
and maybe barking
growling
whining

hmmm....

I think
the moment passed
that moment of dog
was enough
I'll think of dog again
in March.

November 13th
SHORT SHORTS

girls in shorts
long hairless legs
the slightest sunshine
brings them out
and I begin to worry
talking on your mobiles
laughing happy
oblivious to lurid eyes
with dangerous agendas

girls in shorts
I'm not your mum
but sometimes
I see half your bum
emerge
and worry worry worry.

November 14th
DAY MOON

moon in the sky
3pm
broad daylight
to remind us
it's still out there
in the dark and midnight blue
almost round
and laughing at us
in light of day
a trick
the sun will play
with it
to make us feel secure
make us believe
it's all okay
night is banished
safety in the day
then
driving east
you catch a glimpse of moon
mid-afternoon
and remember
where we are
out here
among the stars.

November 15th
MS

my manuscript
stares up gloomily
at me
unread unwanted
smartly bound
and plastic clad
it wants a better sleeve than that
all those words
all those phrases
pages pages
of unfolding narrative
dialogue
plot intrigue
I had some fun with all of that
but if no one gives a rats
about it
as a thing to share
then writing it
will have to do
The End
Goodbye and
toodle-oo.

November 16th
DOW

I wish I cared
about the stock exchange
I wish I understood
its impact
on my life
zero percent
care factor nil
but when I say
I wish
I don't
not really
clearly it exists
within some parallel universe
of sums and numbers
mills and bills and trills
in mind-numbing proportions
graphs jagged contortions
ticking over
hour by hour
and fortunes rise and fall
within a phone call
but how?
but no
I do not need to know
it doesn't interest me
at all
in fact
to think of it
is quite relaxing
not taxing me
at all.

November 17th
CHOCKY

chocolate soft
as plasticene
hard as self-denial
Raleigh's poison for his queen
sweet as victory
lethal as semtex
black as sorcery
tempting as sex
harmful as popery
addictive as crack
cheap as flattery
satisfying as a crap
fragrant as treachery
fatal as lechery
chocolate
o, chocolate
accursed confectionery.

November 18th
PALOMINO BLACKWING 602

slim pencil grey
square rubber at your heel
clipped
in soft metal
guaranteed to
keep correcting
in a flurry of soft crumbs
my thoughts and words
my second guessings
better ideas
shoulds and oughts
instead of
first expressings

sharpened to a flat point
soft wood
carved by blade
will whittle down to stumps
the lead
'til it's too short
for me to grip
the rubber
and the tip
and yet too dear to bin
'half the pressure
 twice the speed'
o, reason not the need
for
Blackwing 602.

November 19th
IDLING

the sun powers down
on my hometown
and I could drink all night
my laziness abounds
my thirst for pink
outweighs the need
for music or a show
I have no will to go
and put on make-up
pick out clothes
re-harness bra
get in my car
and drive
perchance to jive
dig cool guitar
and feel alive
and make small talk
seem so much smaller
with people
who don't know me well
o, well
I guess the telly
is my friend
tonight
and most nights
in the end.

November 20th
ON ERROL ST

last storm of the year?
then it's a good one
flooded roads
heavy downpour
and lightning
thunder and lightning
rare as hens' teeth
in these desert days
of heat and heat
and swollen feet
and sweat
as fat as ice cream
in my hair
send it down, Moses,
love your work
I'm in my car
and dry
and loving it
the cataracts
the steady drip
the wish-wash-wish of wipers
duco gleaming
in the cut and polish wet

sirens wailing
not to catch a fire
I'm not complaining
this could be the last time
for a while
keep on raining
blocked draining
folks refraining
from the urge
to catch a bus or train

last storm?
I hope not
so much pleasure
in the drench
keep it up
send it down
until my thirst
is quenched.

November 21st
BOTS

spam bots
I don't get it
what's the point of them
who wins
who gains
is there a pay-off
money to be made
in pseudo-cyber trade
surely no one answers
we all know they're a glitch
nobody's getting rich
by offering an old woman
sex aids and a bigger dick
and pills
and upgrades to my website
and wills
and friendship
so much friendship
so much love is in the air
but is there really someone
in a room somewhere
in Minsk or maybe Zanzibar
eyes locked upon a screen
a phone
part of a team
in case some fool believes
is ripe to be deceived
by these senseless bots of spam
or
are they merely spores
of poison
the web just cannot trap
moths from @pandorasbox
no firewall can zap.

**November 22nd
MARIOS'**

the café
where I go each day
it pleases me
in many ways
that don't relate to food
or coffee
if I want lunch
I prefer a salad bar
a sandwich
cake shop
ba-na-na

I want company
and sometimes I want none
they serve both
at my café
that's why I go there
every day
to shoot the shit
to chew the fat
discuss the game
dispute the stats
gossip about this 'n that
until the cows come home
to crucify
to praise
bemoan
to gnaw the bone
you can't do that
at home
alone

and crucially
I like my java
hot as molten lava
without needing to provide
a note from my mother
health certificate
doctor's orders
overriding common practise
'barristum contra lactose'
I'd rather drink a milkshake
than a lukewarm cup of foam
with smiley face on top
in brown
a leaf a bird a frown
who looks at what they're drinking
for the art?

the café where I go each day
is used to me
no need to say
I don't need water
ALL THE TIME
or why I am just fine
to sit
and nurse my empty cup
until it's time to pay
be on my merry way.

November 23rd
SKYLINE

drive-in
beneath the stars
John Wayne from our car
Audrey Hepburn panorama
drama
framed by trees
dark sky and moon
while we spoon
across the front seat
smoking
at our leisure
taking pleasure
in comfort of familiar seats
trudging to the kiosk
for some treats
little kids in jarmies
beyond thrilled
to the slippers
half asleep
before the second feature rolls
undulating bitumen rows
of FJs, utes and Commodores
hooked up to speaker poles
so intimate
this communal sleep-out
love-in
au plein air
Lawrence of Arabia
and Ben Hur
technicolour James Bond nights
simple delights.

November 24th
BLOW-UP

Godfrey's clown
is falling down
but no
he's up again
he's dancing slow
to tempt you in
to buy a vac
he won't go slack
so happy
arms spread wide
insane smile
do come inside, folks
don't be shy
don't be like me, he's saying,
all puffed up and swaying
doomed
to dip and scrape
then re-inflate
to his full height
of sheer delight
of suction
cleanliness and power
a tower of nylon
full of air
just as your Volta
Hoover Dyson
will be
when you purchase
eternally on sale
Godfrey's clown
o, Godfrey's clown
top suck of Ascot Vale.

November 25th
MOLLY-ROSE

six minutes -'til you're born
so very long ago
1.12 a.m.
and out you slip
and wail
and I throw up
and shake and shudder
drug torn and exhausted
I'm a mother
and I clasp you scared
against my chest
can't quite believe my eyes
and ears
to hear you cry
and breathe
new air

and your new father's there
in love
in tears of joy
so young himself
a boy
reborn is he
now we are three

today you're thirty-one
and grown
and flown
far away from me
and he
you are
my little girl
and
will forever be.

November 26th
FIRST ONE NOT HERE

well
now it's weird
now the house is empty
and nobody's home
and you're not here
for us to cheer
and wish
happy returns

this morning was all right
business as usual
minus party plans
no cake to cook
dinner to book
the day rolled by
my eyes were dry
but now
I feel the lack of you
the empty
and the vacuum
without you means
on this
your special day
I miss you
and that's all there is
to that
I am your mother
you, my first
and special brat.

November 27th
INTO THE MYSTIC

there is
some fundamental
part of me
that wants to be
spiritual
that seeks
the inexplicable
the bliss
the inner peace
exalted soul
it just won't run to
god
and all that
oogie boogie
antiquation
consecration
transubstantiation
absolution
damnation
and yet
I am drawn
to kneel
to sit
in contemplation
of some higher state
some place to go

but not with any
holy joe
yogi guru
juju voodoo
nor do I seek enlightenment
or specious comfort
in some afterlife
that isn't there
I am not stupid
but
I am aware
of my desire
to walk into a vaulted church
to satisfy some inner need
to gaze upon
some statues
sniff the incense
snuff some candles
tell some beads.

November 28th
DROPPED

the day dawns
when you have to go
false, toxic friend
frenemy mine
nothing in this for me no more
from you
but contempt and scorn
disguised as some kind of
patronage
superiority
fake pal
you have to go
the queue is over there
and it's not very long
but once you're on it
you are queued for life

needy, needy, needy me
can only take so much
opprobrium
before I crack up
jack up
pack my kit
before I see the way
that you see me

it's like a blinding flash
of see-you-round-girl
spotlight on shame
time to cool your jets
take two steps left
time to reflect
life will be a calmer place
if I don't ever
have to see
that snide look
on your face.

November 29th
SPOT CHECK

burned blooded swabbed
job done
health checked
mortality meters read
and logged
standby for results
positive negative
to point the way
steady as she goes
anchors aweigh
live to fight
another day

or

maybes
not-sures
we-don't-really-knows
is your liver
on the nose
I am brimming with confidence
leavened with caution
you never know
'til you go
see your doctor.

November 30th
FINE

pinged!
at the lights
by a second
and an eighth
fate's heavy hand
upon the wheel
of my misfortune
like steel
to the tune of 403
and demerits points 3
is singing
don't relax
pay your tax
face the facts
pay the bills
keep running like a rat
in the spokes
on the grid
because
just around the corner
is the man with the bat
raised to bop you on the nut
when you least expect it
ram you back inside your rut
where you must raise your head

so you run
and you run
so it's Christmas
so what
no fun for you,
rat
keep running on the spot
where it's hot hot hot
while the carnival
keeps spinning
never you that's winning
so you run
and you run
'til you drop down
flat.

December 1st
HANDSFULL

itchy right palm
money in
itchy left palm
money out
seems
I had them
arse about
no wonder I was always out
of pocket
got to read the signs right
or you might
get left out of the scheme
and your dreams
fall apart at the seams
and you stare at your hands
in disbelief
at the sleight
at the treason
at the underhand signals
defying all reason
and belief
what you thought
was relief
was a thief.

December 2nd
LITTLE POCKETS

coins in the tips
of a frock
I like that
something unexpected
in vogue
in retro
wish I had jewels to sew
into those caches
like some intrepid traveller
on a voyage
to the unknown
when the weight
of a penny
wouldn't help
when you drown
2 cents in one corner
5 euros in 'tother
that should keep me
balanced
in my striped cotton pinny.

December 3rd
BIG BANGS

hair tresses mane locks
the difference between
cute and crock
between young and old
a face is not the same
without a frame
born with little
dead with little more
boyish curls
girlish bangs
crew-cut thatch
bouffant bob
chignon perm
eyebrow lashes
shave and wax it
all you like
you will feel the lack
when it is gone
no more cover for your scone
shiny skull cap
poking through
to expose
the real you.

December 4th
NO-ELL

Christmas without kids
isn't Christmas
you were a kid
or had a kid to make it for
without them
it's a chore
a bore
what for?
you ask yourself
magic and surprise
all gone
bring out the wine
the day is long
and no-one can be bothered with a tree
or Christmas cards
we all agree
to forgo presents
or Kris Kringle
when Boxing Day will slash the price
and make us feel swindled
Christmas
it's for kids
it's all about the joy
Barbies for the girls
guns for the boys
it's how you get to learn
the right from wrong

sing silly songs
about snow and myrrh
and reindeers mangers
angel's hair
kings and virgins
partridges and pears
stuff that isn't talked about
throughout the year
without their eyes all full of wonder
Christmas is just a meal we share
wear paper hats
eat too much sugar
pork and beer
and pledge to go AWOL
same time
next year.

December 5th
FRIGHT LIGHT

4.30 light
shears like steel
brighter than a thousand suns
descending in the west
is it me?
I did the test
got my cataracts done
and dusted but
I can't see out the windscreen
sunnies or not
it's not even hot
it's just glare
snow-blindness
blindsiding me like sulphur flare
like Catherine wheels on bonfire night
whiter than the whitest white
million watt globe
lazer cutting to the
frontal lobe
until my eyes are slits
and I pull over to the kerb
to wait out this phosphorescent
blitz
until the danger passes
I cower behind
my useless blue
sunglasses.

December 6th
BLOODY SUGAR

I shall become powerful
like a powerful owl
full of wisdom, wit and charm
I shall thin my blood sugar
on 800cal
my fatty fat deposits
they will melt away
I shall be strong
and play along according to
the plan
no cakes or flan
no spuds or spam
I shall munch so many leaves
I will develop fangs
like Peter Rabbit
no more post-prandial chocolate habit
or buckets full of wine
watch me wax divine
serene
and steely disciplined
retract three chins
and flatten out my chest
resurrect my pins
de-puff both my eyes
until I stand erect
on sinewed knees
to give my feet a break
I will not ache
I shall be reborn
starting from
tomorrow morn.

December 7th
STROKES

a lovely weight descends
from swimming up a storm
limb tiredness
from pushing through
the crystal blue
up down
down up
kick stroke
push pull
turn back

embryonic chlorine home
with just a lick of salt
baptise me
rinse me
float me
in your liquid long wet stretch
of lane
marked out
with bobbing plastic chain
beneath the flapping pennants
of joyful swimming gala memories

diving from the blocks
tumbling turning
beating clocks
fingers hitting walls
in time to beat them all
and gasp
and rip the goggles from my eyes
step up
to claim the prize

in the water
in the pool
I am invincible
I rule.

December 8th
COMMITMENT

o, the river that runs through Egypt
is a lovely shade of blue
it's not chocolate, it's not wine-dark
it is eau-de-Nil, that's true

denial is long and it is deep
and its banks are high and steep
it is cool and clean
and clear as a decision
it will rinse my system out
it will make me look less stout
in just two months
I will be something of a vision.

December 9th
BEER MOTH

behemoth
it's such a lovely word
it's got beer
it's got moth
when you say it right
a moth on beer
seeks out the light
again again
a Kamikaze flight
drunk on lager
this moth gets even larger
gnats and mozzies cower
in fright
faced with the awesome power
of drunken moths
like Facebook

said another way
the 'bee-hem-oth'
sounds like a cough
'harrumph'
'excuse me'
I have got
to knock your block off
move onto your seat
don't argue
I'm in charge
don't bleat

comes from the Hebrew
word for 'beast'
makes sense to me
they have the best words
like
'schlemiel' and 'klutz'.

December 10th
TREES

how can we compete with trees?
artists, sculptors
trees bring them to their knees
jeez Louise
look at those trunks
big spunks
those leaves
those colours
textures
in the dry
we pass them by
their beauty lying doggo
but come the rain
the wet
the water rushing down the plug hole
their palette suddenly
comes alive
like someone switched
the filter up
to hyper-real
surreal they are
wet magic
and each one unique
chuck out your chisels
and paint brushes
throw your easels under buses
we can't compete
with trees.

December 11th
"WHAT'S ON YOUR MIND?"

live by the (s)word
die by the (s)word
you put it out there, big mouth,
expect to get it back
can't hack the crap
along with the shtick
then get out the kitchen, kitty,
quick
before the cupboards
crash on down
and spill the china on the ground
before your smarty pants
could fit a clown
before they drag
your sentence
out to life
for giving it a crack
just for the craick
you dish the dirt, girl,
prepare to cop the hurt, girl,
if I were you
I'd post a picture
of my cat.

December 12th
TANNENBAUM

o, Christmas tree
no Christmas tree
I won't put up the
Christmas tree

the urge is strong
to open up
the box of baubles
angels
apples
stars
and beaded reindeer
collected over time
and duly strung up
strung out
on my own
most years

many tears must fall
as I recall
my bossy ways
with no room for play
my way or the highway
in the art of decoration

ghosts of other
Christmas trees
come back to taunt
the German
the suburban
the natural
and the freshly boxed
from K-Mart
it would break my heart
again
to take part
in this fragile
frosty
snowflake game.

December 13th
HUBBLE BUBBLE

midnight sky
witch flying high
across a woollen crescent
moon
silver tail broom
so light and slender
all witches must be
whippet thin
to straddle such a narrow steed
side-saddle
and to fly at speed
and never lose their hat
my crocheted blanket
freezes her in flight
above a city skyline
cloaked
in dusk
and there are stars
behind below
and afghan squares
to lock the magic in
to catch the spell
up tight
I hooked each stitch
for you, my love,
to wrap you
warm you
through the night.

December 14th
YA LOUSY

it's not easy being green
Gore Vidal
he said it best
a little something of me dies
with every friend's
success
the jobs you should have scored
runs on the board
prestige
awards
that never even saw you
in the running
it shoulda been me
it shoulda been me
you bleat into your G and T
don't start me
on the money

green around the gills
you are
chartreuse
pea soup
absinthe
lime spider
grassy knoll
a cabbage roll
Granny Smith
a cricket pitch
cane toad spitting
acid dripping
bottle throwing
green as grass
with envy
overflowing.

December 15th
PANHANDLING

the world at street level
on your arse
cardboard Sharpie scrawl
on show
so low
we pass you
on the way to Coles
legs of every muscle sinew
shins and soles
what can you read
about us from
our heels
our calves
our knees
which of these
will heed your silent please
you
with your hoodie down
sat all day
watching trousers pass
and swishy skirts
and skinny jeans
ankle socks
knobbly knees
walkers with the means
to spare a buck
give a fuck
take pity on
your lack of luck

but
which stiletto
Nike trainer
is Dr Scholls
a better touch than
Martens
Reeboks
Vans or Chucks
the walking world's
not stopping long
those legs've got some place
to go
they're not stooping low
to drop some sugar
in your bowl.

December 16th
YES

people are sweet
truth is
they get it
mostly
you put it out there
and they're like
yeah
I get that
I see what you're saying
what you're driving at
I see that picture
you're displaying
and I feel the same
as you
who knew
connection
could be
quite so
gratifying
a word
an image
sentiment
or point of view
and suddenly
it's you
on the same page
as people
whom you hardly knew
empathising
in harmony
sweet harmony
universal
interfacing.

**December 17th
UH-OH....**

couch position
glass cushioned
and I am in my cups
the weeks of dry
have shimmied by
now I
have allowed myself
a drink
a bottle
Aristotle would advise
against
my swift demise
to sofa coma
but it's a one-off stay
I shall allow
this disarray
tomorrow
is
another
day.

December 18th
GRIT

I get knocked down
but I get up again
I stay the course
and I give up again
strong in both directions
good and bad
naughty nice
saintly vice
happy sad
honouring intentions
testing out conventions
just to see
how far it takes me
down the road
along the journey
big adventures
curious bold
and when I stumble
on the path
or take a rest from
strictures
I climb back up
wipe my mouth
fix my hair
tie my laces
straighten up
the kid stays in the picture.

December 19th
THE MIST

good will seeps
like mist
through tiny pores
past oak-thick doors
of brick-hard fierce resistance
to the yule
stubborn as mules
we are
but caught up in the dance
of Christmas
we can't resist it
love it
hate it
scorn it
block it
we can't fight the list
of things to do
the traffic
and the drinking
and the drinking
glasses clinking
fuzzy thinking
in the fog
the mist
of Christmas

Santa's juggernaut rolls on
Rudolph's geeing up the crew
Joseph's trudging to the census
God's expecting
His Boy Jesus
Donner Blitzen two by two
reindeer in heaven
camels below
light the star in the east
get this show on the road

and through it all
the mist
the Christmas mist
of mutual obligation
resignation
we are in it
right up to our turkey necks
in tinsel
glazing
pine trees
sleighbells
most folks here have never even seen!
people beam
and wish you merry
and they seem
to mean it
all the way
to January.

December 20th
SANTA BABY

all I want for
X-mas
is my son
and hair
a dog
a job
a meal to share
a book deal
and these poems published
some Linda gigs
a glass of wine
a call from London
cherry pav
and then another wine
to follow
leave the washing-up
until tomorrow.

December 21st
LIKE ME DO

tap Like
that'll do it
tap ♥
nothing to it
problem solved
crisis over
person loved
cold shoulder
the end is nigh
say 'Hi!'
and wave
puppy saved.

December 22nd
BUYING TIME

spending money you don't have
on things you don't need
but want
feels good
feels suicidal
satisfies a
greed
for just an hour
or two
before the shit comes down
once more
to find you
standing
empty-handed
with two bowls
of white and blue
and wondering
what you will do
about the bills
you know
are due.

December 23rd
BRAIN-POD

heads full of song
like mine
must have an outlet
a release valve
through which
some of them can fly
see daylight
hit the air and soar
from out of my vast store
of ditties
bigger than a hundred i-pods
and what's more
I know them all by heart
no cheat-sheets
charts
no cloud required
each note and chorus
remembered for all time

these tunes
must have a little exercise
from time to time
or else
unbidden, there you are
vamping show-tunes
and not just in the shower
you're chanting hymns
at any hour
50s pop tunes
crooning standards
belting blues
clearing rooms
with renditions of some
childhood folk song
bewildered bothered
wondering what in god's name
brought this on
this sudden need
to trill that snatch
relax, you say,
it's just the brain
raising up the hatch
letting a few of them out to play
to keep them fresh
and ready
for another day.

December 24th
THE EVE

we've done all right
Christmas night
food sorted
presents bought and
wrapped beneath the tree
Love Actually on TV
shower and toilet scoured
back yard swept
tomorrow's schedule
firmly in out heads
crack party troops we are
ready for the fray
hip hip hooray
for Christmas Day.

December 25th
A BIT FIT

a tracker for my heart
that's so handy
and for the steps I take
to save it maybe
through daily vigilance
private keeper
constantly on watch
and like a proper watch
it tells the time
the weather
and it clocks
my cals
and how much fuel
I've burned
I plan to learn
a lot about this fleshy unit
I inhabit
how to manage it
more wisely
how to cut it down
a size or two
so fit I'll be
with my new toy
I'll fix my knees
and jump for joy.

December 26th
MIND FAT BODY FAT

my day begins
with thoughts of dinner
what to cook with what
frying pan or pot
cold or hot
chook or chop
to be thinner
I must re-programme
my brain
abstain from morning thoughts
of food and wine
habit of a lifetime
resist the urge to cater
menus rosters
relinquish title of
'chief cook and bottle-washer'

to achieve
a smaller size of dress
I must contemplate
the ways and means
of less.

December 27th
LILY AND GLAD

Christmas trumpets
pierced by horns of scarlet glad
stand browning in the vase
all things must pass
the token branch of pine
is turning beige
time turns a page
and we look forward to another year
scent of lilies
heavy in the humid air
invades my nose like incense
from a swinging thurible
mass
the rosary
time for prayer
these blooms belong in church!
not in my kitchen
they require an altar
statues
chanting
a priest upon his perch
a heady pong they have
those lilies
unlike roses jonquils hyacinth
daphne
ponderous they are
serious
sacred holy
regal celebratory.

December 28th
3 TO GO

the year winds down to
RESET
time to forget
move on
crank the dial around to
GET SET
be ready for another round of
YEAR
fewer of them left now
too early, tho,
to take a bow
just yet
I have a plan
or two
decisions I would like to
ACTION
seek satisfaction
in a course of study
perhaps for money
CONTINUE
in this vein of verse
until the well of ink
runs dry
I have enough to do
to say
to write
to play
to sing
to keep me interested enough
in watching time
RENEW.

December 29th
SMOOCH

a kiss
a little kiss
one that was meant
one that was sent
with love
to me
to the lips
to my lips
for a moment
a stolen moment
maybe
they have the sweetest scent

it's unlikely
no contenders in the running
I can see
still
it would be funny
but not on the money
I may as well
go hug a tree.

December 30th
THE DICK

a year of come-uppance
for the dick
the randy old prick
took a beating
took it lying down
rode it out of town
the old pork sword got sheathed
to cries of 'shame!'
and lawyers ten feet deep
'roman hands and russian fingers'
must learn to play a new tune
in the key of
R-E-S-P-E-C-T
they found out what it means to me
and every other
lady, baby, chickadee
and slut and mole and tart and whore
they tried to start something with
or take to task for what she wore
or take something from
those days are gone,
man,

the cock and bull
the cock and balls
henceforth
must stand up to be counted
powerful campaigns mounted
shaft a spotlight on those dark
and secret places
men with no faces
in the corridors of power
beneath the table
in the shower
the hour has come
for penis power
to cut and run
to take a hike
the town bike has turned
cometh the hour
cometh the woman
with a smoking P.R. gun.

December 31st
THE END

the day draws to a close
a few more hours of twilight
before the last night
of 18
at 18
I could not have cared less
one day is like another
I'd protest
the colour of the sky won't
change
no matter how much gunpowder
they fire at it
from long range
in wasteful bursts
of squander
18 into 19
what's it mean
another chance to dream
to scheme
to hope
aspire
skip rope
perspire
in hot pursuit of higher
standards
new horizons
at the dawn
of tomorrow's sun rising
the world will look
the same.

www.ingramcontent.com/pod-product-compliance
Lightning Source LLC
Chambersburg PA
CBHW061247230426
43663CB00021B/2930